# THE READING FESTIVAL

## MUSIC, MUD AND MAYHEM: THE OFFICIAL HISTORY

### IAN CARROLL

# THE READING FESTIVAL

## MUSIC, MUD AND MAYHEM: THE OFFICIAL HISTORY

### IAN CARROLL

Foreword by Melvin Benn

REYNOLDS & HEARN LTD
LONDON

Published in 2007 by
Reynolds & Hearn Ltd
61a Priory Road
Kew Gardens
Richmond
Surrey TW9 3DH

A CIP catalogue record for this book is available from the British Library.

ISBN 978-1905287-43-7

Designed by James King

Printed and bound in Great Britain by Biddles Ltd, King's Lynn, Norfolk.

# CONTENTS

ACKNOWLEDGEMENTS.............................6
PICTURE CREDITS..................................6
FOREWORD BY MELVIN BENN...............7
INTRODUCTION.....................................8
PRE - 1970.........................................12

1971.......................14
1972.......................18
1973.......................22
1974.......................26
1975.......................30

1976.................34
1977.................38
1978.................42
1979.................46
1980.................50

1981.......................56
1982.......................60
1983.......................64
1984 AND 1985........68
1986.......................70

1987.................74
1988.................78
1989.................82
1990.................86
1991.................92

1992.......................96
1993.......................100
1994.......................104
1995.......................108
1996.......................112

1997.................116
1998.................120
1999.................124
2000.................128
2001.................134

2002.......................140
2003.......................146
2004.......................150
2005.......................156
2006.......................164
EPILOGUE: 2007......170
INDEX.....................175

# ACKNOWLEDGEMENTS

Debbie & Nathan (for letting me get on with it), Mike Horton, Karl Woodcock and Mark Jewitt (the best drivers in the business), Holly and Matt Allison (cat sitters par excellence), Melvin Benn, Tom Ames (Reel Big Fish), Phil Carson, James Sandom (Kaiser Chiefs), Ben Kirby (The Subways), Marc Riley, Hayley Connelly and Kas Mercer (Mercenary PR), Tim Hull (Coors Brewers), Gillian Porter (Hall Or Nothing), Adam Lawrence (for being a phone pest), Tony Nixon (for all the musical inspiration), Angela Davis (Svengirly), David Gedge, Edith Bowman, Bart Dahl (Dinosaur Jr), Owen (Guilfest), Emma Watson (Fifteen Three PR), Tom Haxell (The Wonderstuff), Leander Gloversmith (Velocity PR), Julie Weir (Visible Noise), Ian Gillan, Louise Maine (Mercury Records), Alan Briars (Trowbridge Pump Festival), Sofia (End of the Road Festival), Sharon Chevin (The Publicity Connection), Sharon Rueben (Mean Fiddler), Dave Henderson (*Kerrang!* Awards), Mike (Acoustic Festival Of Great Britain), Roland Hyams (Work Hard PR), Ed Millett (Guillemots), Laura Farrow (Beautiful Days), Steve Zapp (ITB), Liena (Positive Nuisance), Zee & Amy (Love Not Riots), Mark Hamilton (Ash), Linda Petersen (Ted Nugent), Bethan Elfyn (Radio One), John Edney (OPM), Neil Anderson (Biffy Clyro), Anna Brewers (The Agency Group), Linda Serck, Brian Flenniken (Mad Caddies), Lee Noble (Elkie Brooks), Megabus, Peta Blewett (Status Quo), and all the people that I either forgot, or omitted on purpose, due to their attitudes, you know who you are..............?

**PICTURE CREDITS**

Front and back cover photos and all interior photos are reproduced by courtesy of the *Reading Evening Post*, except for pages: 28, 57, 99a, 99b, 121, 125 and 151, which are reproduced by courtesy of Rex Features, and pages 105b and 116b which are reproduced by courtesy of Ian Carroll. All Reading Festival ephemera are reproduced by courtesy of Festival Republic/Ian Carroll. The official Reading Festival logo is reproduced by courtesy of Festival Republic.

# FOREWORD

'**I** am just the keeper of the keys' is how I explained my role to the founder of the Reading Festival when I bumped into him recently. He was asking after the festival's welfare at a function we both attended, and I was pleased to be able to report it was in bloody good health!

The Mean Fiddler (and I) became involved professionally with the festival in 1989, after a couple of disastrous years had left it bereft of ideas and a coherent booking policy – and virtually bankrupt. The then promoter and founder, Harold Pendleton, approached all the 'major' promoters around at the time. They all turned down the chance to be involved. Harold then asked Vince Power, the then-Chairman of Mean Fiddler, who had no hesitation in saying yes. For Vince, an Irishman and founder of the Mean Fiddler club, who barely knew where Reading was, it was a business opportunity of a lifetime and for me it was a dream that had started in 1972 come true.

Seventeen years and approximately 1500 bands later (most of whom have been chosen by Neil Pengelly, our festival booker), Reading is the greatest rock festival on the planet. It has spawned an official sister (Leeds), an acknowledged copycat (Lollapalooza) and dozens of imitators and wannabe's across the globe. I am proud to have been the festival director during that period and the keeper of the keys. But I, and we, are just that; the keepers of the keys. And, while the festival is bigger than all of us as owners, as well as being bigger and longer-lasting than the bands that appear at it, it is – at its core and in a manner that no other festival can lay claim to – a real festival about bands and people who love bands.

The list of bands who have appeared is far too long to mention in a foreword. It is not the right place anyway. In 2007, our company's name changed to Festival Republic. But most importantly, the festival remains as relevant today for the 17-year-old driving from home to see the Foo Fighters or the Red Hot Chili Peppers as it was for me as a 17-year-old hitchhiking down from Hull in 1972 to see the Faces. And it will be as relevant, I'm sure, for the 17-year-old in 2020, space-travelling from home to see their favourite band of the day. And no, it will not be virtual. It will still be in bloody good health and real – if I have anything to do with it. It is its inherent beauty – to be real.

**Melvin Benn**
(Festival Director, Reading Festival)

# INTRODUCTION

The Reading Festival (Berkshire, UK) has been a main fixture of the town of Reading since 1971. From its beginnings outside Reading, in Plumpton, Sunbury and Windsor, to its current home on Richfield Avenue, the yearly event has been a major influence on the UK festival calendar. Other festivals have come and gone, trying to copy Reading's style and appeal, but none have lasted so long. From the early days as the National Jazz and Blues Festival, through the troubled years in the mid to late 1980s, to the present success under Mean Fiddler, the festival has always been held in high esteem by fans and performers alike and has raised the festival to the pinnacle of outdoor indie/rock events.

The festival has grown in stature and recognition, each year adding new developments to improve what has always been a fantastic event. Major improvements took place in 1999 with the introduction of the northern half of the weekend in Temple Newsam in Leeds. The Leeds Festival was initially run one day behind the Reading Festival, with the final day being on the Bank Holiday Monday. This has since changed, and both festivals now run over the Friday to Sunday, leaving the Monday for travelling home. The Leeds festival moved to Bramham Park in 2003, where it has remained ever since.

The other major addition to the festival was the sponsorship of the brewery giant Carling. The company gave the weekend a recognised brand as a sponsor and the festival has become known in the last ten years as the Carling Weekend Reading and Leeds. During this time, it has gone from strength to strength, with the line-up announcement being eagerly awaited by music fans all the world over.

When I first considered the idea of writing the Reading Festival book, I fully expected to find that it had already been done. My research failed to turn up any such competition, which immediately encouraged me to pursue the idea. Why, I thought, does the vast rock audience not have access to a chronicle of the success of this major musical event? As a music fan who has attended the festival since 1983, I believed that it was time a book was written about one of the highlights of the UK festival calendar.

From July 2004 I started to compile notes about the festival from my collection of programmes and other memorabilia. I then began the task of contacting bands that had played the festival from its early days as the Jazz Festival to recent years. From August onwards, I started to receive extremely positive responses from various artists. The majority of these responses resulted in contributions of experiences. I then contacted bands via their management companies, PRs and record labels and interviewed them in person. Sometimes this was an easier approach because either (a) many artists either couldn't be bothered or didn't have the time to sit down at a keyboard and bang out a piece about their festival experience, or (b) they didn't have a computer to 'bang one out on' anyway!

From this point the phone calls started coming and I spent many hours in the kitchen, speaking to Alice Cooper, Scorpions, Bjorn Again, Francis Rossi, Twisted Sister and more. It's a hard life, but someone had to do it, thank God it was me! From travelling to Florida to interview the Editors, to walking to my local venue to interview Kaiser Chiefs, it's been a long and enjoyable journey and I've travelled many thousands of miles in the process, but here we are at the starting point of this *Rock 'n' Roll Year Book*, and I welcome you, one and all, to THE BOOK of the Reading Festival.

Ian Carroll, July 2007

# PRE-1970

The National Jazz Festival began in 1961 at Richmond Athletic Ground, the festival being the brainchild of Chris Barber and Harold and Barbara Pendleton, owners of the Marquee Club in Soho, London. Throughout the 1960s the festival flourished, growing each year, with the venue moving to Windsor Racecourse in 1966, Kempton Park in 1968, Plumpton in 1969, and finally making a permanent move to Reading in 1971. Bands that appeared during these years included The Rolling Stones, Spencer Davis, The Who, the Yardbirds, Joe Cocker, T Rex, Pink Floyd, The Move, Al Stewart, Jeff Beck, Deep Purple, Jerry Lee Lewis, Traffic, Yes, Black Sabbath, Cream and a host of traditional jazz bands.

'We played with Deep Purple in 1970, in Plumpton when we set fire to it – I mean the stage accidentally caught on fire.'
**Ian Gillan (Deep Purple – Vocals)**

'The Reading Festival was the final outcome of a festival held in various places (almost entirely due to local authorities not enjoying the notoriety nor the inevitable disturbance to their tranquil way of life!). It was founded by Harold and Barbara Pendleton and myself (all of us being the owners of the Marquee Club). It was first staged at Richmond Athletic ground, where my band was a top-of-the-bill attraction and The Rolling Stones performed in the impromptu club setting in the clubhouse.'
**Chris Barber (Chris Barber's Jazz Band – Trombone)**

'I played the Reading Festival just once if I recall... I'm sure I did in 1971 or 1972, but I really couldn't swear to it. In a nutshell, festivals were just great "get togethers" back then. Everybody helped each other out, everybody felt like they were headlining and the audiences came to hear everybody.'
**Rick Wakeman (Yes/Strawbs – Keyboards)**

'I first went the year The Crazy World of Arthur Brown performed. I have a vague memory that a fire broke out near the stage as he was singing "Fire." The next time was probably in the late sixties, when a lot of the British blues acts were becoming popular. Ten Years After played in the days when there were heated discussions about whether a guy who could play a hundred notes a second was better than a guy who played a few and made them count.  But my main memory of that show was when Jethro Tull appeared on stage and Ian Anderson balanced himself on one leg and the crowd went wild. Me and my purist friends were disgusted at the audience's reaction to such crass showmanship, when they had treated the great Stan Webb and his purer blues with much less interest.'

**Graham Parker (Graham Parker & the Rumour – Vocals/Guitar)**
'What eventually became the Reading Festival started off in the early sixties as the National Jazz and Blues festival at Richmond, Surrey and moved to Kempton Park race track soon afterwards. I played there in 1968 with Tramline, a band from my native North East (Middlesbrough).
We supported Traffic, The Spencer Davis Group, John Mayall's Bluesbreakers and an unknown outfit called Jethro Tull. They blew everybody off and went on to… In 1970 I joined Juicy Lucy. We were scheduled to play the festival, though I don't remember the location. Never got to play because bands like Yes and Deep Purple overran. Bastards!'
**Micky Moody (Tramline/Juicy Lucy – Guitar)**

'It was the first big gig we had played (10,000 people) and I remember how thrilled we all were to be there. We got a standing ovation and an encore and I think that gig was a major point in the band's career. I was so excited and can't recall much about the backstage goings on, except to say that we carried on the party later that night at the Speakeasy Club in London.

'We came back from our first US tour to play the 1968 Festival and we were on a high. Our *Undead* LP was in the US charts. It was all happening for us. We'd started doing extended jams in the States and our 45-minute set on that day was only one long number, 'The Boogie' , where each band member took a solo. It was self-indulgent and could have left us with egg on our faces, but we got away with it. We played "I'm Going Home" as an encore.

'Many bands had been to the States and a number of us had brought back fringe buckskin jackets and cowboy hats, etc. The musicians, crew and management in the backstage area looked like a bunch of extras from a western movie. The Nice

augmented their lineup with some Scottish Pipers.'
**Leo Lyons (Ten Years After – Bass)**

'I was surprised a couple of years ago to see a poster from the, I think,1968 festival, with us top of the bill, over all the big names. I do remember the Windsor Festival in 1967 when I caught fire, but I'm not sure if that counts as an early Reading one.'
**Arthur Brown (Crazy World of Arthur Brown – Vocals)**

'I remember playing with the Herd; we were second on the bill to Jerry Lee Lewis. We'd done a couple of songs and part of the scaffolding fell down and went straight through the drumskin!'
**Andy Bown (The Herd – Keyboards)**

'I remember seeing an awesome bill headlined by Cream – who were amazing – and PG Arnold and the knife. It was a very memorable experience – PG Arnold kept stabbing an organ with a knife. He kept stabbing it and kicking it and taking an axe to it, I think. I had never seen anything like that at the time and as a 16-year-old at his first rock concert I was quite wide-eyed.

'The other artist I remember from that festival was Arthur Brown, who had a hit at the time called "Fire". He swung onto the stage on a rope that was on fire and used a lot of fire on stage; it was pretty outrageous for the time. The whole event created quite an impression on me – in spite of the fact that I was not high on anything.'

# 1971

**After spending several wandering years as the nomad among festivals, travelling around various accommodating areas of Berkshire and the home counties, this was the year that the festival finally took root, found a home and established itself in sunny Reading, where it has remained ever since.**

'I really don't have any memories of either of the Reading Festivals. Must have been doing too much stuff!'
**Arthur Brown (Crazy World of Arthur Brown – Vocals)**

'I must confess that over the years one gig blends in with all the others! I seem to remember the band Yes backing up US jazz singer John Hendricks at an early Reading Fest, but I can't recall if I was there as a punter or if I was working.'
**Steve York (East of Eden – Guitar)**

'It was our very first big festival, with a lot of acts who have since become "giants". Funnily enough, because it was more heavy rock, we thought that we might not fit in. We went on stage, some young people started throwing things, but when we started our first number people seem to stop and think "what's coming now?". From then on everyone was grooving, which was nice. The day that we played it didn't rain, so there was no mud!! After that it did us good and we realised that we could fit in anywhere.'
**Teddy Osei (Osibisa – Vocals/Saxophone)**

'The first time I played the Reading Festival was in 1971, with Rory Gallagher and Van Der Graaf Generator. There were many pop bands.'
**Gerry McAvoy (Rory Gallagher Band – Bass)**

'As a young musician growing up in Reading it was exciting news for us when the jazz, rock and blues festival came to town. The festival was bigger than anything we could have hoped for. It had its doubters amongst the local residents and traders, but nobody complained about the revenue it brought to the town.'
**Mick Kirton (Groundhogs/Dumpy's Rusty Nuts/
Hawkwind – Drums)**

'We could always hold our own with the other four/five piece bands, even though there were only two of us. We could kick out one hell of a sound, I played bass drum, hi hat, guitar, and harmonica, and Peter Hope-Evans was such a huge presence, along with his percussion, jaw's harp and mouth bow, he played the most heart-felt harmonica you ever heard, a real shout from the soul. People would say they could hear choirs, orchestras, the full metal outfit, because those were the seeds we were sowing as we played and melted into the audience. It was a true spiritual experience.
'We always had a great intimacy with our audience, always a great connection, they totally identified with our closeness to them. We were playing in the rain, but I recall that as we kicked into "Pictures in the Sky", the rain stopped, and the sun came out!! We all soaked up the warm rays.'
**John Fiddler (Medicine Head – Vocals/Guitar/Piano/Drums)**

'It was our first-ever tour of the UK, the 12 of us plus wives, girlfriends, roadies, plus Uriah Heep and Paladin and their wives, girlfriends and entourages, all in one large motorcoach. We made our way from Southend to East Kilbride and back, and many was the late night when the chant of "LITTLE CHEF" would fill the bus, since it was the only food available.

'I remember vividly noting that on our itinerary it showed Reading to be 40 miles from our London base... For some reason the coach call was 9 am, which evoked much grumbling. Four hours later we pulled into Reading. Although it rained the entire way up, it seemed to clear a bit as we pulled into the festival grounds. There was one large shed backstage that was the communal dressing room and green room. The festival goers were quite soaked and well-lubricated, and got into the spirit of our performance like the "Teds at heart" that they were. Having played Woodstock, Reading did seem to be the UK equivalent, granted without the half-million people. It was a once-in-a-lifetime experience... real rock 'n' roll fans revelling in the music and the scene.'
**Screamin' Scott Simon (Sha Na Na – Piano)**

'Reading's proximity to London ensured that the backstage area would be crammed with loads of folks who just came down for the lig and never saw the stage or the audience. The entire membership of the Speakeasy and La

RIGHT:
Arthur Brown – conventional is not his middle name

BELOW:
Culture clash at the shops

Chasse clubs would be in the backstage bar and we usually had friends down from the north for the gig. The net result was that we would have a hugely enjoyable social occasion that would be interrupted for an hour or so while we performed.'
**Ray Laidlaw (Lindisfarne – Drums)**

'I know I wore my new leather coat that my manager Jo Lustig insisted I buy. And amongst other songs I sang one called "Michael In The Garden". This stuck in my mind because on the evening news, when they mentioned the few drug arrests, they showed pictures of the festival and in the background you could hear Yours Truly singing with an acoustic guitar. I thought it strange that they illustrate the great rock festival with a guitar and vocal instead of a big rock sound.'
**Ralph McTell (Vocals/Guitar)**

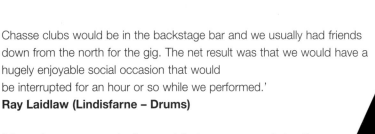

'Although we were billed to play in 1971 and we were there all ready to play, the festival was running late and there were some serious backstage meetings going on as to who was going to play and who wasn't. Unfortunately, Stray drew the short straw and we did not actually play! While our managers Peter Amott and Ivan Mant were backstage trying to sort this out, I remember sitting right at the front of the stage with Richie Cole the drummer of Stray and with Andy Byrne (who later went on to drum with Dirty Tricks and Grand Prix). We watched Osibisa and stamped our feet so hard in the dirt (Osibisa were very percussive, don't you know) that we'd made a big furrow where we sat. We also watched Coliseum, who were really good. We had a truck load of dry ice which we now could not use. It was dumped in the river to melt ... except it caused a huge mist or should I say "Smoke On The Water"!'
**Del Bromham (Stray – Guitar)**

'In 1971 I was 17 years old and had been fortunate enough to have been brought up in a family where music was an essential part of our everyday life. My Mum was, and still is, a great Frank Sinatra fan and my brother Jeff and I followed the traditions of that era and listened to The Beatles, The Kinks, The Rolling Stones, Cream, Bob Dylan and the Beach Boys.

'I had desperately wanted to go to the Isle of Wight festival in 1970, where Jimi Hendrix was headlining, but my mum told me I was too young. It was then that a festival came to Reading. My friends and I only had to walk from our homes to the festival every day, and could sleep in our own comfortable beds at night, luxury! If I remember rightly, tickets for the whole weekend were £12.00... if only they cost that much now! Sometimes I hear mention of a long-forgotten band, and it takes me straight back to those fantastic carefree times.'
**Jo Bate (former Reading resident)**

RIGHT: Camping seventies style

A mixed crowd

# 1972

Ray Dorset of Mungo Jerry loves to play at Reading 'In The Summertime'!

18

**The second year at Reading was again a great success and the festival was now officially called 'The National Jazz, Blues & Rock Festival'. This was the year that Status Quo became popular, the 'love tent' opened, selling condoms to the masses, and other 'copycat' festivals were taking place all over the country. But none could match the festival in Reading.**

'The Reading Rock Festival holds dear memories for me. Being a festival day, as Vinegar Joe, we set out to enjoy ourselves in every way we could and took to the stage that Sunday afternoon with a youthful exuberance and a harsh determination to give the rockiest, raunchiest performance we could. Being on stage with Robert [Palmer] was always a pleasure, as he was an astonishing talent and so good looking in his youth. There was a real musical connection between us. I still miss him.

'We must have gone down pretty well, as I remember reading a great review, and seeing myself on the front cover of *Melody Maker*, or *Sounds* magazine the week after. The atmosphere from the crowd and camaraderie between performers was magical that day, and a real positive vibe was felt by all. I don't think I will forget the experience of performing at Reading (especially the toilets!), and feel privileged to have been part of such a legendary rock festival.'
**Elkie Brooks (Vinegar Joe – Vocals)**

'We'd played three festivals in those weeks in Lincoln, Wheely and Reading, and each one has been quoted as the one we broke from!

It was all starting to come through for us; we played in the 6pm slot and it was fantastic because it was in daylight. From that day on we realised that playing to a large outdoor crowd like that, we're much better in daylight. A lot of bands like to go on at night, but then I can't see the crowd and it loses a lot. So that time we played it was really phenomenal.

'I remember when I came off I saw Don Mclean and said to him "what a blinding record" ("American Pie") and he just went "hummmhhhh", I think he had the hump about something. I think Peter Gabriel had just shaved his hair funny at the front and as he walked past he grabbed me on the cheek and went "uuuuuhhhh". It's funny things that you remember, but he was quite friendly.'
**Francis Rossi (Status Quo – Vocals/Guitar)**

'I was not really looking forward to doing the gig; this was the first UK high-profile show that I was undertaking since the line-up change of the band. We had a rehearsal of sorts some time before the day of the show, mostly jamming, as that was what we were about – I never really stuck to a particular set

list – and made arrangements to meet at the festival site. A few days before the gig I was driving around the Bracknell area, listening to John Lennon's *Imagine* album so intently that I failed to spot a police speed trap and I got booked for speeding, so I announced to the audience that they had better watch out for the police when they were in the area as I had "just got done for speeding". They let out rip-roaring cheers and applause – I guess that they had assumed that I had been "done" for the amphetamine type of speeding.

'I don't actually remember many of the songs that I played. I did play "Gimme Dat Harp Boy", a Captain Beefheart song that I used to do with the previous line up, and I think that it was Julie Burchill that wrote that I had a cheek to play it. We finished off with some rock 'n' roll which had the audience on their feet and I think that it was Mark Plummer writing for *Melody Maker* that gave us the only good review for the show.'
**Ray Dorset (Mungo Jerry – Vocals/Guitar)**

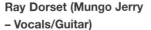
Peter Gabriel of Genesis sporting his very individual 'runway' haircut

'The fans were the most knowledgeable I've encountered. However, little did they know that ten minutes before showtime, Keith Moon had just spent 30 minutes playfully scrapping with anybody daft enough to take him on.

'Whilst on stage with Jackson Heights, during a quiet few bars, I let a botty burp loose and the crowd were so silent and appreciative it was heard way at the back by a Hells Angel who yelled to my embarrassment... "WE MAY NOT PLAY BUT WE KNOW A BUM NOTE WHEN WE HEAR IT."
**Brian C Chatton (Jackson Heights – Keyboards/Vocals)**

'My biggest memory of this year was the outfit I wore on stage. Influenced by the mirror balls I had seen time and time again in the Mecca ballrooms and clubs around the country, I decided to make a suit of mirrors so that when the lights hit, literally hundreds of shafts of light beams reflected from me!

'So I put the suit on backstage and when I went to get on stage, it was then I realised that I could not bend my knees enough to climb on. So a couple of my road crew had to lift me onto the stage. I think we went on at about 6pm, so naturally in August it was nowhere near dark enough to get the full effect. Fortunately for me as I recall, the weather was quite dull and within the confines of the stage, when the lights went on, the suit of mirrors did what it was supposed to do!'

**Del Bromham (Stray – Guitar)**

'A real landmark for us, our introduction to the "big-gig" thing. A sea of people and bright sunshine. Just the job. We did an afternoon acoustic set and it went well. When we came off we had a quick chat with Peelie (God bless him), probably about football, and recalling the time when he once gave the young, skint, hitch-hiking Sutherland Bros a lift up the M1. A good man!'

**Gavin Sutherland (Sutherland Brothers
– Bass/Vocals)**

**RIGHT: John Peel contemplates the future of British rock
BELOW: Preparing for the festival – cars and campers**

'I will always remember Rod Stewart in his leopard print suit, strutting his stuff, and when Status Quo were playing, the crowd held up thousands of tiny lights, from lighters and matches and candles, creating a magical scene. I've described the scenes so much that it sounds as though the music was of little importance, but the bands and their music were of course the essence of the whole weekend and an integral part of it. I just remember so much more about the whole event and hope that other people enjoy remembering these things too.'

**Jo Bate (former Reading resident)**

READING FESTIVAL ALE BY COURAGE

# 1973

**Now a permanent fixture in Reading, the festival was back for another year. The Faces gave their final 'farewell concert' in Britain over the weekend and the sun shone over the site. More rock bands were now being added to the bill and the festival was no longer jazz orientated.**

'The backstage drugs were different in those days – Watney's Red Barrel instead of Stella Artois [!].... But rock music is equally deafening in all its incarnations.... I played the festival a few times – always at the mercy of the weather. I recall it was so bad for a Genesis show we had to pull out... of the mud, mainly.'
**Steve Hackett (Genesis – Guitar)**

'A year later we were back for what we call "toppo", "toppo de bill". When you're young, you're desperate to be at the top of the poster and all the shit. But, the older you get, you don't care where you are as long as you get on, get on early and sod off!

'We played in darkness and there was a massive pit and the audience was 60 feet away, so it lost that vibe. So if the first one had helped break us, it could have been the second one that helped finish us!'
**Francis Rossi (Status Quo – Vocals/Guitar)**

'I always hate to be useless, but I'm afraid I only went once, back in 1973. All I remember are The Faces... and mud.'
**Paul Gambaccini (Radio 2 Presenter)**

'We had played a few small festivals before, and earlier that year had played the massive Long Beach Arena in Los Angeles, as part of David Bowie's Ziggy Stardust tour of the States, but this was Reading, and that sense of being part of one of the world's most famous music events really started to kick in. As we arrived at the artistes' entrance to the site and passed through to the backstage area, the excitement and anticipation grew. A mini village had been created for all the artistes, sound and lighting crews, record companies, invited guests, journalists etc.

'As we acclimatised to this surreal new world, I wandered around with my wife and son to see what was going on. It has to be said that the hospitality tent was a world within a world. All the drinks were free and the journalists, record-company guests, agents, managers and general hangers-on were making the most of it!

'I bumped into John Peel (who was drinking coke) and he wished us luck for the day. Quietly spoken and articulate, he shared his own feeling of awe at the "Reading experience" which calmed my own emotions a little. Our roadie Tubs found me and said it was time to get ready for our performance, we were on stage in half an hour! Here we go then, this is almost it. We got changed and went over last minute reminders regarding the set. Jack Barrie, Marquee club boss and co-organiser of the festival, had popped in to tell us that this gig was gonna make us and best of luck.

'We mounted the stairs to the festival stage and with every step the excitement and nervousness grew. I can't remember who it was that introduced us, but it seemed to take forever. "Ladies and gentlemen, hippies, boys and girls, READING, please welcome on stage Fumble." We strolled on waving (as you do) and started to play, in my opinion, one of the best gigs of our life. The adrenaline had boosted us but not completely taken over and we rocked till we dropped. By the time Sean hit the first notes of "Nut Rocker" we had nigh on 20,000 people on their feet and leaping in the air. To stand in front of a sea of humanity, all clapping and bouncing and dancing and smiling, was a memory that will stay with me forever. I cannot

Chilling out seventies style

possibly put this feeling into words, indeed I would have to be a poet to get close. But by the time we finished our set I floated back to our trailer on a cloud. Hugs all round, and a very impressed six-year-old son, if not a little confused by it all. Does Dad really go out and do this ALL THE TIME?

'We took an age to wind down from our incredible high, and when we did we wandered again around the backstage village. We played Frisbee with Lindisfarne in the hot sun for quite a time, I remember that. My son approached the legendary Keith Moon from the Who (who was only there as a guest, and unfortunately not performing) and told him he was barking mad! Keith asked who had given this young innocent the message and he pointed to his dad. With a wink and a raise of his glass, it was the only time we were ever "introduced"!

'Whilst I was chatting to our pianist Sean in one of the backstage hospitality tents, we heard the opening few bars of "The Twelfth Of Never" by Donny Osmond! What!!!!! Nothing against the chap, but Donny and Reading, especially with this track, did not

**Festival goers relax between bands**

go together at all. It was John Peel at the turntable – how could this be? A peculiar sound – 20,000 confused revellers scratching their heads and grunting and wondering why the mood had changed from more appropriate music festival fayre – it really was tangible.

Mucking about in the river

like syrup from Donny's lips "and that's a long long tiiiime" a couple of seconds past when the opening notes to "Layla" SCREAMED through the Reading sky. The place went ballistic! We had popped our heads out front to soak up some of the atmosphere and witnessed just about the whole of the festival responding to Mr Peel's artistry. He had taken them all to a place of calm and safety and numbness, then with Eric Clapton's classic track had unleashed a whirlwind upon them! The crowd punched the air, levitated, screamed, dropped to their knees, kissed each other, and demonstrated all instincts of ecstasy.'

'By the time that Rod Stewart and the Faces finished the evening I was in a tired, but gloriously satisfied mood. It had been a long, long day filled with excitement, and nervous energies, filled with hope and expectation. And we had been rewarded a hundredfold with the experience.'
**Des Henly (Fumble – Vocals/Guitar)**

'At the time I was quite friendly with Mell and Slug, who were Status Quo's road crew. I remember me and some friends meeting them at the band entrance and getting in for free. We sat in the press enclosure, right in front of the stage,

and saw Quo give an excellent performance.
This was at the time that they were really breaking through in the rock world from their pop early start. This is the great thing about Reading; the fact that if your music is worthy of greater things, playing to such a big audience can certainly help you break and encourage extra people to come to your provincial gigs.'
**Mick Kirton (Groundhogs/Dumpys Rusty-Nuts/ Hawkwind – Drums)**

'It was our first major festival appearance, and living up to Lindisfarne's reputation was a little daunting. As it turned, out we need not have worried and the gig went extremely well. Two of the members of JTL were always up for a spot of mischief and after an hour or so in the backstage bar post-performance, they set off looking for some fun. I don't know who instigated it but a short while later they joined another band on stage (I think it was the JSD Band) dressed only in outfits made from

*Rod Stewart keeping the Scottish end up, with the Faces*

24

cardboard boxes. This unannounced and unexpected appearance caused much hilarity on the stage and much confusion in the audience.

'The two chaps, who should remain nameless, then toured the site blagging drinks from all and sundry and paid for them with IOU's written on bits of the boxes. The end result was two almost naked and very drunk musicians careering through hospitality until they collapsed in a heap on a nice little lawn outside the Warner Bros

tent. They slept there for a couple of hours while the great and the good stepped over them to access the freebies.'
**Ray Laidlaw (Jack The Lad – Drums)**

Jack The Lad in action

# 1974

**The 'Rock' Festival had arrived, with Lizzy, Alex Harvey and Heavy Metal Kids leading the assault. The near 'non-appearance' of 10cc caused them to be fined a 'substantial proportion of the total fee' by Jack Barrie, after appearing on stage 40 minutes late.**

'I simply cannot remember anything at all about Reading Festival 1974... I wonder why!!'
**Eric Stewart (10cc – Vocals/Guitar)**

'Perhaps it was the abundance of chemical refreshments back then, but I can't recall playing the Reading Festival, at all.'
**Kevin Godley (10cc – Vocals/Drums/Percussion)**

'My first experience of the Reading Festival was in about 1974. I'd been to a couple of Hyde Park gigs with the Stones and Floyd, but it was the first proper festival I'd been to. I was working with the MAM Agency at the time and, if I remember right, I had Cockney Rebel on the bill.'
**Rod Smallwood (Chairman
– Sanctuary Artist Management)**

'At the end of a mammoth, sold-out European and UK tour, only weeks before the festival, three of the original members walked out on me. I was left with a band comprising a rhythm guitarist/singer (me) and a drummer, Stuart Elliott, the only one to stay the course. And, of course, through recruiting new faces with a sort of "the-show-must-go-on" mentality, my career and my life took a totally unexpected u-turn: until then, Cockney Rebel had had no lead guitarist. Now I brought in Jim Cregan on guitar and for the festival we signed up as substitutes Francis Monkman on piano/Hammond and Herbie Flowers on bass.'
**Steve Harley (Steve Harley and the Cockney Rebel
– Vocals/Guitar)**

'I'm afraid I can't remember too many details of the few times we played, as much as I try. I know we went down really well both times and managed to get the crowd on its feet, whereas most of the other bands were pretty laid back.'
**Keith Boyce (The Heavy Metal Kids – Drums)**

'It was a very interesting bill. Despite sharing the same record company, I don't remember seeing Cockney Rebel, but I had enjoyed Focus's albums and so it was a pleasure to be on the same bill as them. I think we played well and the set list was almost certainly the same as on the *Barclay James Harvest Live* album. If we were hot, then the festival was not, for it rained and rained, thereby inspiring me to write a song on 1999's *Nexus* album, called, appropriately enough,"FESTIVAL!"'
**Woolly Wolstenholme
(Barclay James
Harvest – Keyboards)**

'Even in our massively elevated status as the penultimate act on the Friday, it was not the same as '73. Whilst we still had huge nerves and a fabulous response, it didn't have the innocence for me of that blistering day the year before. We had arrived late afternoon in '74, as we were not on till late in the evening, and there were lots of people "looking after" us. Playing in the evening has a far more dramatic effect than in the day, visually speaking. The lighting rigs come into their own, as the banks of lights can be seen for the first time through the darkened sky. And a different atmosphere is created. You can't see the huge crowd, because of the thousands of watts of lights that are shining in your eyes, just 20,000 halos around a sea of silhouetted heads. Remarkable though it was all the same!

'A memory of this year was 10cc not being there, as time for their appearance grew nearer. Their manager was suggesting to festival organiser Jack Barrie that if they didn't turn up in

Reach for the stars!

Steve Harley

time, Fumble could take over their spot and they could play after. "If they are not here in time" he said "they do not perform at all! The Reading Festival is bigger than the sum of its parts and will not be manipulated." Nice one Jack!'
**Des Henly (Fumble – Vocals/Guitar)**

'I was partnered by Graham Cooper, guitar, and we had been touring with Focus, the Dutch group. The gigs had gone very well, and we'd played in Europe with them to. For some mad reason we two guys with two acoustic guitars followed Steve Harley and Cockney Rebel, before Focus came on to finish the night.

'We were supposed to have a piano but that had been put on the wrong stage. I remember we did everything at a frantic tempo, a couple decided to have sex in front of the stage and a lot of torches were lit. It was quite bizarre. I think we were the only people on that hadn't had a hit record of some sort. However, the crowd were forgiving and we left the stage intact and without injury. Graham remembers standing next to Rod Stewart in the pissoire and being unimpressed.'
**Harvey Andrews (Harvey Andrews – Vocals)**

Frisbee Championships of the World 1974

# 1975

**The crowd this year was the biggest so far, with the police trying to keep the people off the streets and by doing so, boosting the crowd to near 50,000 – when the licence was only for 30,000. The rain poured and the Saturday night headliner, Yes, took to the stage 65 minutes late. Reading was now the biggest festival in the country.**

'It rained and poured the whole time. We were not only wet, we were drenched, and my amp short circuited, so I had to play with a practice amp I had, which was a very small Fender super amp that was not grounded very well and every time I went up to the microphone and sang, I got an electric shock. Apart from that I couldn't hear my own guitar or anything, so I was playing blind, and was getting soaked to the skin and I can't even remember who else was on the bill.'
**Roger Hodgson (Supertramp – Vocals/Keyboard)**

'The Reading festival was the first of its kind for Priest and for that reason alone the concert was a very memorable one! After working so hard for so long, it seemed as though we had finally arrived in a world of rock giants, playing alongside the likes of UFO, Thin Lizzy, Supertramp and Hawkwind!! Hanging out backstage was a real blast – I can remember the atmosphere was electric – and when Hawkwind hit the stage the vibe was surreal. The festival at that point could have been taking place anywhere in the universe – it was great!!'
**KK Downing (Judas Priest – Guitar)**

'Reading Festival was always considered to be one of the most important ways to break a new artist, back in the seventies and even into the eighties; it probably still is for all I know, but then I'm getting old! To get the right slot was never easy, Jack Barrie was very careful about who he'd put on and where. Generally speaking, they would want people who had done well at the Marquee and then he would give them a good spot at the festival.

'Which he did with Yes, who were one of the first bands to break out of the Marquee, where they were given a Monday night residency for several weeks and that really "broke the band". I had a very good experience with the Reading Festival and the Marquee with Yes; they were both events that really established the band for me, back in the seventies.'
**Phil Carson (ex head of Atlantic Records)**

'I was a strong fan of Wishbone Ash, whose set I remember as if it was only last week. All that day it was very dark and overcast but as soon as Wishbone came on to the stage the

Harold Pendleton on his 'new fangled mobile phone contraption'

clouds parted and the sun came out. No, it wasn't something that I had swallowed, it actually happened!!!
The other thing that I can remember so well was the plainclothes police trying to dress like hippies to infiltrate the so called druggies; you could spot them from a mile off!!!

'Oh and people going around collecting money for the "Bust Fund", as the local magistrates court was overflowing with drug fiends being nicked for possessing a bit of weed. My how things have changed since those days!'
**Dumpy (Dumpy's Rusty Nuts – Vocals/Guitar)**

'I first played [at Reading] with my jazz/rock/afro/cosmic dream sequence band ZZEBRA. I decided to drive there myself and of course my clapped out Ford Zephyr died on the M4. Total panic ensued – on stage in two hours, wife and five-year-old son in tow, luckily for me our then manager Laurie Adams came along and delivered me and family in style to the backstage area at Reading, a quick drink, and we are on....

'My memory of the gig is pretty hazy – it was that sort of band, a continuous jam session on tour. I think the weather was good and it was the biggest audience I'd ever played to back then. Most of the audience were dancing (remember that?) – we went down well. Little did we realise that in years to come Steve Byrd, Liam Genockey and myself would be back on the same stage with Ian Gillan and Colin Towns playing the first gig with Gillan.'
**John McCoy (Zzebra – Bass)**

'There is some soundless film of this. Don't remember too much about it. Our keyboard player Tim Hinkley was pissed off with the Heavy Metal Kids for making a pass at his wife. Stoned days.'
**Micky Moody (SNAFU – Guitar)**

'We played fairly late on the Saturday afternoon. I think SNAFU, Thin Lizzy, Judas Priest, Wally, and Kokomo were also on the bill.'
**Bernie Marsden (Babe Ruth – Guitar)**

'It was the end of a gruelling European tour (called "Startrucking", put together by our manager Miles Copeland, along with a host of other artists), and the road crew wanted to finish off with a bang. During the encore most of our trusty helpers – male and female – filed out on the stage in front of us and mooned the

**Who needs a campervan? Hippies in the boot**

JWG 268E

SINGER

audience. They had stuck letters on their behinds
(two apiece!) depicting the name of our current album –
C-U-N-N-I-N-G-S-T-U-N-T-S.'
**Mike Wedgewood (Caravan – Bass)**

'I went to see the Mahavishnu Orchestra. The band above
them were Alberto Y Los Trios Paranoios, they were a comedy
band and absolutely terrible. I was watching John McLaughlin
playing this sublime "jazz fusion" and then this bunch of
clowns came on afterwards and I thought that it was one
of the worst pieces of judgement I've seen in my life!'
**Henry Harrison (Mystery Jets – Guitar/Vocals/
Keyboards/Percussion)**

'I went with my best mate Graeme, whose dad was
ex-army, and he packed us off with a full survival kit
(including tinned provisions, a camping stove and bottle
of butane gas). Everything was fine in the early part of the
day as we sat watching the bands in glorious sunshine, so
we decided to kick off our army issue boots and spread out
our sleeping bags as a blanket and generally relax into the
experience. Bad move! Having never been to a festival before
(or a bona fide gig if you discount seeing Showaddywaddy
at the local Palais) we were unprepared for the hysteria that
greeted the arrival of Hawkwind when they took to the main
stage that evening.

'The crowd swelled to three times its size in an instant,
sweeping us along a good 20 feet from where we'd foolishly
pitched camp. Trying to reason with acid heads and bikers
as Stacia stripped and mimed skinning up onstage was nigh
on impossible and suffice to say we were parted from all our
worldly goods before you could say "Orgone Accumulator".

'Wandering around the festival site after they'd played their
final encore, I managed to find one boot. We spent most of
the remaining time that weekend sleeping under the tent flap
of a bunch of lads from Bristol, who had a seemingly endless
supply of scrumpy.'
**Gary Marx (Ghost Dance – Guitar)**

**BELOW: A sea of people and flags**

# 1976

The long hot summer of '76. Droughts, standpipes and hose pipe bans. This didn't stop the rain on Saturday night, which flooded the site and caused the usual muddy mess. This year featured the only festival appearances of rock legends AC/DC and Ted Nugent – the biggest crowd pleasers on the Sunday.

'I remember Van Morrison and Dr John being at the side of the stage when we played. We'd done a festival in Germany in the afternoon and we'd flown back in a private plane and we actually flew over the site, which was fantastic.'
**Gerry McAvoy (Rory Gallagher Band – Bass)**

'Supremely throttled by one of the finest R&B&R&R bands ever, Cliff Davies on drums, Rob De La Grange on bass, and Derek St Holmes on rhythm guitar and vocals, my intense musical dreams were on fire, certainly that day. Performing my American black-influenced soul music for the first time to a gung-ho audience in a country that produced The Rolling Stones, The Beatles and Yardbirds, and who woke up the world to Muddy Waters, Howling Wolf, Robert Johnson,

Little Richard, Chuck Berry, Motown and all my black heroes, I felt a distinct connection to the emotional primal scream that surely brought us all together at Reading.'
**Ted Nugent (Ted Nugent – Guitar/Vocals)**

'My business partner Andy Taylor and I also had a small catering company called "Party Chef" around that time, and we did the backstage catering at Reading around the '76 –'77 period. I was cooking burgers and driving the van!!'
**Rod Smallwood (Chairman – Sanctuary Artist Management)**

'The record companies would take marquees and we'd decorate them as best we could. When I was running Atlantic we had a marquee, with a little garden out the front and a little shrubbery. As technology improved, they brought out a video system where the journalists would stay in the bar and watch the acts and carry on drinking, but not give a shit really!

**LEFT: As busy as ever**

**BELOW: The crowd 'chill out' in the sun**

'What you really wanted to do was to get them out there to watch a band and it made it a little difficult to do when they were having such a nice time on a summer's day! I remember that I had just signed AC/DC six months before and Jack had put them on, not in a great slot, and it was when they had two stages. In those days I used to work a lot with Led Zeppelin and whenever they appeared at a multi-act concert there was always a very strict rule "no one else is allowed on stage when they are on stage". So I went to their manager Peter Grant and asked if I could hire a couple of Zeppelin security guys and ended up with about four. They all came down and I said "look lads, we're going to put AC/DC on, but I want to exert the Led Zeppelin Rule, with the Led Zeppelin authority, and I don't want anyone onstage when AC/DC are. I want you to be as you are, but doing it for this unknown band from Australia." So they said "no problem, squire" and of course it worked like a charm.

'I'd taken over lead vocals from Mic Rogers, a wonderful singer and guitar player. The high point of the show when he was in the band was a Bob Dylan song called "Father Of Night", which involved finger picking a very solid guitar part and singing. I was finding this song particularly hard to sing, and even harder to play the guitar part. I do actually remember being worried about playing Reading, as we would be playing in daylight. I think the gig had been going okay but nothing spectacular. As a band we relied a lot on vibe and atmosphere, and I think we were struggling a bit. Well, it came to "Father of Night". I began to play the picking guitar part, and stepped up to the mic to begin singing the lyrics.

'AC/DC tore the place up and the journalists stayed for the whole set and they were an incredible group back then, and they still are of course today. But a couple of days later I got a very irate phone call from John Peel, who said "what went wrong at Reading, why wasn't I allowed on stage?" They'd actually thrown John Peel offstage, which was a mistake because he was the only person who played AC/DC records back then, which he stopped doing immediately, of course!'
**Phil Carson (Managing Director – Atlantic UK)**

'At that point there was a crack and flash of lightning, followed almost immediately by a massive roll of thunder. I just kept on singing to this great light show in the sky, it was fantastic. Eventually it started to rain quite heavily, but the people stayed because it was somehow magical with that piece of music. Finally, after a long guitar solo accompanied by lightning and thunder, we finished the song as the sun came out.

Never to be repeated!!!'
**Chris Thompson (Manfred Mann's Earth Band – Vocals/Guitar)**

'I had to drive down from Yorkshire, and owing to the weather/ traffic, only managed to arrive a few minutes before we were due to go on. To my surprise (after all, I knew I was going to arrive), there was much consternation and Brian Eno had already managed to plan a set to be played without me...'
**Francis Monkman (Phil Manzanera's 801 – Keyboards)**

'There were about 50,000 people (all wearing blue jeans) and about half the crowd did not want to hear reggae, these people had signs up saying "F'off ". They were the rock fans.

'While we were on stage, a fight broke out between the two groups, bottles and beer cans were being thrown around, but we just kept on singing until we had an encore. Cans and bottles were going on stage, but we kept on singing anyway. We had a lot of friends there to support us.'
**Lloyd 'Judge' Ferguson (The Mighty Diamonds – Vocals)**

'I had a call from the late Ron Apery of Back Door. "What ya doin' this Saturday?" "Nothing'." "Fancy doin' a gig in Reading?" "OK."
He picked me up early afternoon and stopped at a few pubs en route. I didn't bother asking about the venue, expecting to play at a Jazz Club or maybe the university (Back Door were quite a highbrow Jazz-Fusion band). It was only when we turned into the festival site that I realised that I was about to blow in front of tens of thousands of people! That was the seventies for you. The gig went well!'
**Micky Moody (Back Door – Guitar)**

'My most salient memory of Reading is of the moment when I thought that the music biz was definitely changing in a way to which I wasn't at all sure I gave my support, even half-heartedly. I'd wandered around out front for a while in the usual mud bath and lo-ratio toiletage; on returning backstage I came across a hairdresser's, for that crucial last-minute pre-stage tonsorial touch up. Two worlds dividing here dramatically, I thought.'
**Peter Hammill (Van Der Graaf Generator – Vocals/Piano)**

'What I mostly remember is the press reaction and their reviews. As Camel were a band that the audience loved and the press hated, the reviews came as no surprise: *Melody Maker*: "Camel, who appeared later, need a crash course in what makes rock 'n' roll rock!." *NME*: "Camel were inventive, thoughtful and slightly boring." And my personal favourite, *Sounds*: "Next on were Camel, who I found inordinately dull. The guitarist's facial expressions throughout the set suggested he might have a sharp toothed rat down his trousers, but apart from that, they seemed visually and aurally most uninteresting." Despite the reviews, we went down a storm. We had a fireworks display, which was meant to go off at the end of the set. The crew, however, started lobbing bangers at the band during the last number, so we were hopping about, dodging

explosions. We might have been boring to the press, but they couldn't say we weren't animated at the end of the show.'
**Andy Latimer (Camel – Vocals/Guitar/Flute)**

'We were with our old chums Quiver. Deep joy! A big crowd of people and a lovely, happy vibe about the place. Can't remember anything else, we partied rather seriously in those days. Hope I didn't offend anyone!'
**Gavin Sutherland (Sutherland Brothers and Quiver – Bass/Vocals)**

**LEFT: The aftermath**

**BELOW: Down on the campsite**

# 1977

This year again featured amazing 'special guests' on the bill. From the USA there was Aerosmith and the Doobie Brothers, plus, on the Friday, Golden Earring from Holland. Also, as punk rock was now everywhere, the Damned were banned from playing the festival, in true punk rock style. The weather was amazingly bad, possibly the worst ever, so wellies were the order of the weekend.

'It was so long ago that I played there with Heep; it is a bit of a blur. I can remember one of the days, but that's about it. As far as I can remember, it was good.'
**John Lawton (Uriah Heep – Vocals)**

'Intoxication: to bring together in a single place and body, to mass troops in a place; to fix one's attention, energy on a single object; to intensify the strength of a substance or liquid by evaporation or purification; to come together round a single centre, to mass in a single place; to exercise intense mental effort, to focus all the intellect on one point; to devote oneself entirely. This is what the Reading Festival is all about....

'Reading came and went. SAHB blew the place apart. And on the day there were fleeting moments of genius. We may even have been scornful, getting swept around like a bunch of immoderate drag queens loving every minute. Ah! Yes! Reading. In spite of which fame in the end proved to be little more than intoxication.'
**Zal Cleminson (The Sensational Alex Harvey Band – Guitar)**

'When we played there I recall feeling like quite the star to be included on the bill. The festival, to me, meant that you'd really made it, and it was only the second year of my career. Our show was made special by the fact that at some point the power died and I quickly got the audience into an impromptu chant: "Turn the Power On! Turn the Power On!"'
**Graham Parker (Graham Parker & the Rumour – Vocals/Guitar)**

'I played with Frankie Miller's Full House to a good reception. Also on the bill was the Sensational Alex Harvey Band (Alex was crucified at one point in the set!), the Michael Schenker group and the Doobie Brothers.'
**Micky Moody (Frankie Miller's Full House – Guitar)**

'I first appeared at Reading in 1977, as unscheduled backing singer with the Sensational Alex Harvey Band!'
**Philip Chevron (The Pogues – Guitar)**

'Interesting what difference a year makes. In '77 we were down the bill and it was all so-so at the start – but there was a heavy presence of Marquee and other freaks, so the crowd soon got infected.'
**John Foxx (Ultravox – Vocals)**

'I played the Reading Festival three times and each was a very different experience. The first was our biggest gig to date and is now mostly a blur.'
**Warren Cann (Ultravox – Drums)**

'For some time I thought, what will be interesting to do at Reading? – as everyone seemed to look the same, a bit like it's hard to find a Goth who looks unique. So I had the bright idea (one watt at most) to perform as the Grey Man, my hope to express being an individual. I dyed a leotard grey, I painted my guitar grey, I got grey make up, but I didn't tell the others of this plan. What can I say... it wasn't at all popular with the band. It was a good laugh from my point of view. I think in the end I had to use a white fretless precision bass, as the paint didn't dry on my guitar.'
**Chris Cross (Ultravox – Bass)**

**John Foxx of Ultravox charms the masses**

The late, great Phil Lynott of Thin Lizzy, lets rip with a blistering bass solo

'Reading was a milestone for the Hot Rods as a band, and also for me personally, as a couple of years earlier I'd been there as a punter for Hawkwind. Also on the bill was UFO, who I was to join as bassist some ten years later. I was 18, and we had the most unenviable slot going: first on in the afternoon. In true festival style it had pissed down with rain the night before, and all that morning. I remember this for one reason and one reason only. Standing at the side of the stage, probably with a few whiskies and God knows what else in me lingering from excessive partying the night before, I just wanted to get on. I figured a casual stroll on was out of the question, so holding my bass aloft, fondly thinking I would make a bit of an entrance, I made a dash for it across the stage.

'In that high-tensioned teenage state, I'd neglected to take stock of the fact that the stage was still very slippery with rain and mud, despite being furiously swept by the crew moments before. About half way across, running in my shiny new winkle pickers, I felt myself slide inexorably backwards… Falling heavily on my arse, I went one way and my bass went the other. 30,000 people pissed themselves laughing, but I was oblivious to it, my cool blown. I scrambled up, briefly registering the rest of the band trying to stifle their mirth, grabbed my now out-of-tune bass, and headed to the front of the stage.

'Afterwards, I did my first *NME* interview. I called The Stones and The Who old farts. They'd have been in their late twenties [sic] at the time. Ah, the sweet arrogance of youth!'
**Paul Gray (Eddie and the Hot Rods – Bass)**

'In years gone by in '77, when I thought I was macho and hitch-hiking was the norm for crossing the country, I embarked on my annual pilgrimage to Reading. There were three of us, two not used to hiking, I the seasoned campaigner. They would hitch as a pair and I would take my chances alone. Their forfeit would be to take the tents and sleeping bags, and I would travel light.

'No sooner had I started my trek from Tecalemit Roundabout in Plymouth, thumb barely raised, I had secured a lift and lo and behold the Reading skyline beckoned a mere four hours later. Darkness soon fell, the temperature dropped, goose pimples erupted but my friends with tent and sleeping bags were nowhere to be seen. It was 3.00am, no roof over my head, no pillow to cradle and without my nightly Horlicks I wondered how was I to survive?

'A young lady passed, noticed my predicament of only the stars for company, and in a softly-spoken voice offered assistance and I was invited back to her tent with her dozen friends or so. She was an angel indeed, I knew I was too young to die of exposure, dehydration or maybe even starvation, though it must have been at least 12 hours since my last meal.

'The kind-hearted angel and her travelling companions had trekked from Southend-on-Sea and gladly shared their tent for the night. The darkness soon became morn. And a new dawn was born. The tribe cordially invited me to share breakfast with them, my taste buds jumped for joy at the thought of perhaps sausages, fried eggs and maybe even a rasher or two of smoked back bacon and a mug of tea. The fire was lit, the pan was warming but no sign of food, the tribe were on their knees, I gave a startled gaze as they chased insects, juggled worms, clasped beetles and squashed ants that piled into the fryer.'

'My hunger was replaced by fear, the speciality of the day – not my favourite cuisine, bugs delight!!! With a rapid loss of appetite I made my apologies and with haste was gone for ever from their lives, gladly to return to starvation, dehydration, nausea and only the elements for company. Alas – 24 hours later I was reunited with my two companions, my sleeping bag and tent.'
**Paul Paskins (Reading Festival Vegetarian)**

'I decided travelling light was preferable and set off in my pumps, with just a sleeping bag and a heavy-duty bin bag to protect me should it rain (which it did the whole weekend). I managed to stay drunk throughout the festival (my pints and chasers phase) and came round just long enough to pogo in the mud to Ultravox and see Alex Harvey play one song.'
**Gary Marx (Ghost Dance – Guitar)**

LEFT: Scott Gorham of Thin Lizzy

RIGHT: The late and greatly missed John Peel

BELOW: 'We'll sit this one out!' The crowd relax in the summer of '77

# 1978

**Punk rock arrived at Reading for the first time in the form of Chelsea, Penetration and the Tom Robinson Band's 'punk rock lite', among many. But the majority of the chaos over the weekend was caused by the skinheads who came to see Sham 69 and the stage invasion that took place after Jimmy Pursey taunted the crowd with 'If you don't like it, fuck off!'**

'The Jam weren't a festival band but we played Reading. It was awful. I went straight from Reading on holiday to Cornwall. The following week the *Melody Maker* front page read: "The Good, (Johnny Kid...), the Bad (The Jam) and the Ugly (Sham 69)." I prayed no one would recognise me with that headline!'
**Bruce Foxton (The Jam – Bass)**

'What a difference a year makes. All the tours had sold out and we got the all-time attendance record doing a resident fortnight in Soho, at the Marquee. It got so dangerous, the GLC slapped an injunction on the club, sweat was cascading onto the equipment; it was all strobes, howling feedback and beautifully twisted audiences. Danger of Mass Electrocution, not that anyone would have noticed. So a lot of that carried over into Reading. Stage sound was chaotic, but that was how things always were. The entire scene was changing over from Punk to Freak at that point. But at festivals the rate was slower, and some of the audience were still Rockist. The stage crew was definitely Rockist. Audience mixed, still quite a few surviving moustaches looking sideways at the Spikes. Weird. We hadn't seen daylight for quite some time and were definitely not compatible with it. Second time was much better, since we were next to last on the bill. Bit too much lighting though, I like to hide. Good colours, all red and electric blue, but no strobes. A nicely epileptic strobe was essential. I remember thinking everything was a bit blurred, and then I realized it was me.'
**John Foxx (Ultravox – Vocals)**

'I was proud to be there and pleased we were on in the evening because, of course, the stage would be bathed in lights and much more dramatic.

'The audience was pretty vibed up and we appeared to be going down well. I was enjoying the excitement of it all, and then about halfway through our set, things started getting rowdy. Okay, no problem, we'd come up through nights at the Marquee that the police and Fire Marshall had fits over. Punk was going strong and this was reflected in the acts and the audience. We were already playing through a torrent of gob, though most of it wasn't actually reaching us due to the height of the stage. I could see it as the lights caught the trajectories against the black of the night. With the reflection afforded by years, I'm sure everyone looks back amazed that spitting on the band was actually considered a compliment at one time. This disgusting practice started in the clubs and carried on from there. It quickly morphed into something else altogether, and a lot of people used it as an excuse to be an arsehole.

'Then the cans and bottles started. Perhaps frustrated at not reaching us with spit, people had turned to an abundant source of more substantial ammunition. You can throw a bottle farther. I mean, it's physics, innit. For once, I was glad to be at the back of the stage and somewhat shielded by cymbals and mic stands. The rest of the band appeared to be ducking the stuff but the overall mood had changed rapidly. I was wondering how far this was going to go before someone came to their senses. Then our singer, John, got clocked with a can of lager someone had decided to not bother drinking before throwing. I could see his scalp bleeding and blood was running down his face. "This is crazy," I thought. "Surely we're out of here!"

**LEFT: Sham 69 prior to the riot**

Ian Gillan screams for Reading

'To John's credit, he stood there and took it. He must've figured "What the hell, it's just a cut. Might as well make the most of it." He carried on and the photographers were having a field day, as he threw lead-singer rock martyr shapes, augmented by the extra spice that only real blood can provide. We finished our set and then got out of Dodge. Can't remember if we did an encore. Somehow I don't think so.'
**Warren Cann (Ultravox – Drums)**

'The festival came just after my first hit "Cor Baby That's Really Free". My show has always been pretty theatrical. I remember climbing up the scaffolding to the top of the stage and being followed by the sound crew, who had to climb up and pass me a microphone. We played mid afternoon. The mixed reaction we had was summed up by the music press. *Sounds* had a banner headline running across a double-page spread: "CRAZY OTWAY SIMPLY MAGIC", whereas the *NME* had half a column inch something along the lines of "there will always be people stupid enough to enjoy an act like Otway's...."'
**John Otway (Vocals)**

**BELOW: Some people just get carried away**

'We were pretty green at that time, hadn't really been on a bill with any big names, so one of the first surprises was the "hospitality" area for the bands. We just had the use of a basic portakabin 15 minutes before and after our set, whilst Patti Smith had one with her own garden and water feature! Wow, the rewards of stardom!

'Being the first band on has its pros and cons. Being first on means we got some sort of basic sound check... BUT we got to play the first song as everyone was streaming through the gates! In spite of that, to this day, I still get people saying they saw ATF at Reading.
**Peter Banks (After the Fire – Keyboards/Vocals)**

'We managed to attract a fair amount of beer cans and some bottles too – it was hostile, to say the least. But we ploughed through our set without too much trouble. It kept us on our toes; poor Glenn was rooted to the microphone and couldn't dodge the onslaught, the trials of a lead singer.

WE ARE HERE

READING ROCK '78

'Jools, however, turned up late, in fact he missed the first 20 minutes of our set, we all went on in bad moods and hoped that somehow he would turn up by the end of the show, which he did. Glenn gave him some cold looks and the rest of us tried hard not to have eye contact with him, it was a tense old afternoon. At the very end we went to walk off stage to the dressing room, all fairly sweaty and pissed off, and a little bruised, Jools was already in his car and leaving the site with his girlfriend Mary. In the dressing room we all felt cheated by his attitude, but in hindsight it was very rock 'n' roll of him.'
**Chris Difford (Squeeze – Guitar/Vocals)**

"It was punk's first appearance at the festival. I remember arriving there and being allocated a caravan as our dressing room. Seem to remember Fred wrecking the caravan. John Peel introduced us on stage some time in the afternoon. Terrible sound but we just had to get on with it. Seemed to go okay.'
**Pauline Murray (Penetration – Vocals)**

'It was a beautiful day, we spent quite a bit of time hanging out backstage with John Peel and various other people and then Steve Hillage turned up, who we'd all forgotten was supposed to be coming on stage to play "Kids Are United" with us. If you've ever seen the video of us at that year's festival you may have wondered why "Kid's Are United" completely fell apart in the middle. I think we must have all been off our faces – before going, on Steve had asked each one of us individually where in the song he should play his solo, unfortunately we all gave him a different answer.

'As we were in the middle of recording, we couldn't hang around too long after the show, but were told later that some of our more unruly fans had managed to get backstage and let all the record company execs' marquee's down whilst in mid drink. After that we were banned for life from ever playing the festival again.'
**Dave Parsons (Sham 69 – Guitar)**

'Ian had been offered an early spot for the now defunct Ian Gillan Band, so he asked us if we should form a permanent band and do it as the first gig! A frightening first gig, with little rehearsal, but the adrenaline kicked in and we went down well... and we continued to appear at Reading for the following four years. Thankfully moving in the right direction up the bill.'
**John McCoy (Gillan – Bass)**

'We were on just before Status Quo. We were about half way through our set and doing well (I thought) when the crowd started chanting something. To me it sounded like "Go! Go! Go!" I went over to Steve Wright, my bass player, to see what was going on. I said something like, "I think they like us." Steve said, "Are you nuts? They hate us!" I couldn't understand what the crowd was chanting at that point. I thought it was something encouraging (I was just a rookie then).

'Well, it turns out that we were being shouted off the stage by the Quo Army and they were chanting "Quo! Quo! Quo!", while we were doing our introspective love songs. To make a long story short, we left the stage early that day, our heads hung in shame. Looking back, we had a great time at the Festival, drinking beer backstage and raving it up with the music press (who were quite encouraging to us). I'll never forget my baptism by fire at Reading'
**Greg Khin (Greg Khin Band – Vocals/Guitar)**

**BELOW: Entrance to the festival**

45

# 1979

With the late cancellation by Thin Lizzy, the German metal band Scorpions were drafted in as a late headliner, off the back of their 'Lovedrive' World Tour. The American rock contingent were there in force with Molly Hatchet, Nils Lofgren, Cheap Trick and more; but the festival debut of The Ramones was not meant to be, with them and After the Fire pulling out at very short notice.

'We were touring with *Lovedrive*; we were on tour in the United States, our first American tour. Our manager called us and said "Hey guys, you're supposed to be the headliner for the Reading Festival." We said "Okay, we have to do that."

'We arrived one day before and the next day we were going on stage. For me the whole show was like we were in a different world!! Our sound man and the lighting guy had problems because of re-routing the board and the lighting board, it was a very, let's say "risky situation". The English guys they were really experienced. Some of the first German festivals were disasters. In North Germany there was a festival where they burnt down all the equipment, but in England it was already much better, everything was really prepared.'
**Rudolph Schenker (The Scorpions – Guitar)**

'Before we went on stage we got really pissed. I have this show in good memory since many of my English friends came to see me. (Remember I lived in England from 1971 until 1977).'
**Herman Rarebell (The Scorpions – Drums)**

'I knew the booker, Jack Barrie, who was also the booker for the Marquee, and it was he who set me on this course of doing the Reading Festival. I remember playing a few shows at the Marquee and saying "what do you think of the band, Jack?" as I respected his opinion – still do. After the place closed he said "I am going to put you on at Reading this year, early on in the day and we'll build you up, it'll be great." It ended up being a glorious sequence of events.'
**Ian Gillan (Gillan – Vocals)**

'I was the proverbial young gun, I had joined Gillan a few months earlier, and that was like a dream come true. And then came Reading: I was a bit scared, I'd never done anything like that, I'd no idea what it would be like, we were on in daylight, no lights, not easy to shine through: but, I was going to do all I could to have people notice me, I knew the band at its best was unbeatable and at its worst was extremely beatable!

'I drove down with Mick Underwood and his wife Sue and a female friend of theirs, whose name escapes me; I remember it was the first time I ever saw a cruise control setting on a car. Hey, those were the days! I'm not good company coming up to a gig (my wife would probably say I'm not good company ....ever!), I don't much like talking or being talked to in those situations, so for me it was a bit of a stressful journey, I probably did a lot of grunting.

'We got there and into the mobile changing room thingy. I was stressed to fuck, but the rituals of stage clothes and tuning always help, and a quick beer. At the time I hadn't really any say in the set lists, but they always seemed to suit me fine anyway. I remember Jon Lord popped in, lovely man, real gentleman, don't remember if it was before or after, or both! And David Byron of Uriah Heep popped in too. Nice guy too, a bit wrecked.

'And then the usual Reading thing, no sound check, on with a wing and a prayer, just turn both my stacks up full and hope for the best, go crazy, jump around, stay close enough to the drums to be able to hear the hi-hat and snare and you're okay. End of the first number, "Secret of the Dance" or "Sleeping on the Job", can't remember which, you don't know what the reaction will be, it could be an awful silence, but it was just one huge roar of approval: the audience just loved us. Don't let 'em finish, hit them while they're down, straight into the next track. From then on it was easy and I don't remember any of it other than feeling on top of the world.'
**Bernie Torme (Gillan – Guitar)**

'We had had personnel changes and the line-up was Ian, Colin, myself and new boys (!) Bernie Torme and Mick Underwood. We had just released "Mr Universe" and were flying high... particularly me ... I was the first person to "fly"

**RIGHT: Lemmy of Motorhead – firing on all cylinders**

ABOVE: Scorpions as last minute replacement headliners

ABOVE: Wilko Johnson, full steam ahead!

at Reading.... My memory is clouded by the immense pain in the crutch/groin/balls I suffered while being hoisted far above the Reading stage and left hanging! The guys controlling the hoist thought I was having such a great time! Still, I learnt how to "fly" properly after that, and did so where ever venues allowed!'
**John McCoy (Gillan – Bass)**

'I'd written and arranged all the music and some of the lyrics, so it was a big moment to step on stage (the usual scary – is everything working? Are the monitors okay? And the "out front" sound?) and go down a storm with songs no-one had heard before, apart from "Smoke on the Water" of course. It was the beginning, for me, of the Gillan band.'
**Colin Towns (Gillan – Keyboards)**

'The first time the band ever played "Walking in the Shadow of the Blues" was at this gig, recorded by the BBC, if I remember rightly. We were about halfway down the bill, and Peter Gabriel was headlining, his manager arranged for him to play before us, drastically changing the running order – a big mistake, as it turned out. Halfway through his performance, which I watched and enjoyed very much, the Snake fans began a chant for us, the roar increased by the minute. Peter ended his gig early. Whitesnake was becoming very popular.'
**Bernie Marsden (Whitesnake – Guitar)**

'As I remember, we were on due to our performance at the Marquee Club. One of the managers, or owner of the club, was so impressed with our performance that he insisted that we were put on the bill. Well, after a most stellar performance the press wrote, and I quote "Inner Circle is the only band that did not play for their pockets."

'The following morning we drove to the airport with the driver who drove Cheap Trick back to London after the show and he told us how surprised those guys were and how they kept asking who we were and where we were from. I guess that was the first time people realized that there are many different styles of reggae.'
**Touter (Inner Circle – Keyboards)**

"I played with a pal, Zaine Griff. I'd met him through Hans Zimmer and loved his music. He was offered a spot at the festival and needed a drummer, so I was happy to stand in. Another reason I took the gig was because Hans was playing

synths in the band. He and I were planning projects of our own, so this was a comfortable fit and promised to be fun. 'On the day, I was poncing around in our band tent with less than half an hour to go before stage time. I was feeling pretty good; I was a Reading vet by now. Hans was backstage preparing his gear. Suddenly, he dashed in looking absolutely pale. He whispered "I can't get the sequencer to load! I've tried absolutely fucking everything and it just won't load!!" Not wanting to panic everyone, he'd kept his remarks only to me. I froze. Now it was my turn to turn pale.

'The magnitude of this disaster can't be overstated. If we couldn't fix it, we'd be completely screwed. At least half of the songs in the set revolved around sequenced pulses and there wasn't a hope in hell to get the material across without them, they were written that way. Hans was using a big chrome ghetto blaster as his portable cassette deck. The leads went from Audio OUT to Audio IN. "Have you checked these leads?" "Yeah. Three times! Nothing." "Are you sure the cassette is good?" "I've tried them all. Still nothing." I stared at the bloody thing, running all the options.

'Tick…tick… tick… No pressure, right? The band was not going to like this. I just keep staring at the boom-box, not so much in concentration as desperation. Then I saw it. The source of the solution glowed faintly for a second, like in the movies. I said, "Uh… maybe you should try this" as I reached over and gently flipped the silver toggle switch from RADIO to TAPE. We just looked at each other for a moment, stunned at the absurdity of it, then tried to not laugh too hysterically. We might not have been able to stop. Our jangled nerves not withstanding, the gig went great and we prudently refrained from mentioning this little episode until later.'
**Warren Cann (Ultravox – Drums)**

'We were the first band on the first day. Just turn up, throw your gear on the stage and get on with it. There was plenty of people there. We had a good time.'
**Steve Carroll (Little Bo Bitch – Guitar)**

'The best opening band I've yet seen at Reading. A good tight pop/rock outfit (featuring one Steve Carroll).'
**(Lee Burrows – Praying Mantis Roadie)**

**LEFT: John McCoy of Gillan with his trademark haircut**

# 1980

This year is remembered for Slade tearing the place apart. As a late addition to the bill, to fill the slot made vacant by the cancellation of Ozzy Osbourne's Blizzard of Oz, most of the crowd didn't even know that Slade were appearing. They were the most popular act all weekend and this performance re-launched their career and saw the chart hits start up again, including the 'live' EP recorded on the day. This year also saw the New Wave of British Heavy Metal start to make an impact on the line-up, with Def Leppard, Iron Maiden, Praying Mantis, Girl and more playing over the weekend.

'I will not have the time to do it the justice it deserves.'
**David Coverdale (Whitesnake – Vocals)**

'It was a glorious gig, one of the last of the great Reading Rock gigs; we arrived in a fleet of very flash white limousines, and had a very big end-of-tour party at Jon Lord's house. George Harrison was there, we had some exotic dancers, one of them sat on George's lap, the entire room sang "She Loves You". Happy days.'
**Bernie Marsden (Whitesnake – Guitar)**

'We had two warm-up shows and then into Reading. I had such a good time that night, although it was daunting because I was the "new boy"

and I had the entire Chrysalis bigwig contingent staring at me from the side of the stage! The crowd were great if I recall and the group were on pretty good form. We played a couple of tracks from *The Wild, the Willing and the Innocent* which was being recorded at the time.

'Prior to our appearance there were three large balloons spelling out "U-F-O" and I have been told by our school chaplain (who quite bizarrely was in the audience) that "U" sailed off in another direction, leaving the message "F-O" to the crowd! I think that sort of sums up UFO's luck really!'
**Neil Carter (UFO – Saxophones/Keyboards/Vocals)**

'It was Ted McKenna, myself and Rory. Nine Below Zero had played an amazing gig that day and everyone was a bit frightened after it, as we were going to be on last. It was a good festival, though.'
**Gerry McAvoy (Rory Gallagher Band – Bass)**

LEFT: For Marc Storace and Krokus, Swiss time wasn't running out!!

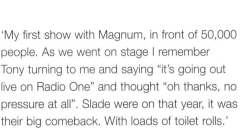

'My first show with Magnum, in front of 50,000 people. As we went on stage I remember Tony turning to me and saying "it's going out live on Radio One" and thought "oh thanks, no pressure at all". Slade were on that year, it was their big comeback. With loads of toilet rolls.'
**Mark Stanway (Magnum – Keyboards)**

'Slade were asked at the last minute, three days before the show, as Ozzy Osbourne had dropped out. We hadn't done any live work as a band for almost a year. Dave Hill didn't really want to do it. As far as he was concerned, we had broken up.

'Chas Chandler (our manager) got Dave to do the show saying, "at least go out on a high note!" Finally, we all said yes!!!!!! And rehearsed for three days, like mad!!!!!!! We turned up at the site not even being billed, we had to park in the public area (and pay for parking), as we didn`t have any passes. We trundled through the mud backstage, trying to find a dressing room which hadn't been allocated, with people saying to us: "What are you doing here?" There was no hospitality for Slade. We purchased our own drinks and food from the outside vendors. The rest is history – so the saying goes!!!  We went on stage! Stole the show!! The concert was amazing for us!!!!"
**Don Powell (Slade – Drums)**

'I went with David Byron (Uriah Heep) a few years in a row... Total VIP treatment, as you can imagine. I've got many great memories, like... one year a famous actress called Britt was backstage when this guy ran up and (gently) nibbled her left breast. Mild amusement all round... After the show I was driving David's roller home when a cop car fell in behind us... then another and on and on until at least five police cars and two bikes were tailing us.

'Substances in the glove box were consumed as fast as possible...panic ensued.  David was frantically directing me to smaller and narrower roads. Eventually the blue lights flashed, we were ordered from the car and surrounded by a small (quite large… fucking massive actually!) army of plod. Then out of the blue (as it were) the officer in charge recognised "Mr Byron". "Sorry sir, thought your Rolls Royce had been stolen, I do apologise for stopping you, please continue on your way, have a very good evening."

'Relieved, exuberant celebrations ensued all night. Back on site the next day! That same guy was back, wearing a t-shirt proclaiming "I Bit Britt's Tit"...nice one! Like everyone, I saw some absolutely great bands at Reading… but Slade gave one of the very best performances I was lucky enough to be there for.'
**Robin George (Magnum – Guitar)**

"We were special guest to Rory Gallagher, who headlined the Friday night. I knew we'd go down well; it was just a matter of how well. All I remember of it was how cool it was in the dark, with spots panning on the audience and lights and torches out for what looked like miles: it looked totally utterly stunning from the stage, like the Nuremburg rally on acid with rock music. All I remember about the gig is that we played "Trouble" for the first time in front of a big audience. It hadn't been released yet, far as I can remember. We had played it a night or two before at a warm up we had done, maybe Aylesbury Friars, I don't remember. Anyway, we did it at Reading and it was like wow, the whole place, 30,000 people, was bouncing up and down, and they'd never even heard it before, I can remember clearly thinking as we played it "if this isn't a hit nothing ever will be."
**Bernie Torme (Gillan – Guitar)**

'We were whisked straight off stage and off to a private plane to make an appearance at a festival in Germany. Saxon were on and Ted Nugent. We were knackered and the useless hired equipment ended up being trashed or thrown into the audience! The crap organisation at this and many other festivals made you realise how good it was at Reading, and how things ran relatively smoothly.... But it's all pretty much a pleasant haze after all this time. At every Reading we (and other selected bands) were treated to the sound of some nutter with an air horn that he would let rip usually at the end of a song, or a remarkable solo, but worst when he was bored or didn't like something.... He became known to us as "ARRY AIR ORN".
**John McCoy (Gillan – Bass)**

'We went on stage dressed in all our Mod suits and we were pelted for the first three numbers with coins, rubbish, mud and beer cans. Then we decided to do "I Can't Quit You Baby" and they recognised that we were linking Blues with Rock and from there on we went down an absolute storm. We had only just signed to A&M records and recorded the *Live At The Marquee* album, but it wasn't out by then. But we went down so well that they invited us to come back the next year.

'I also remember all the record company doing drugs in our caravan. We were really innocent and they were the rock 'n' rollers. They were all coming out with gear on their noses and we were thinking, what are they doing in the toilets?'
**Dennis Greaves (Nine Below Zero – Vocals/Guitar)**

'New guitarist Steve Carroll fit Mantis really well, helping the band get back the "heaviness" missing since Pete Moore's departure. Mantis was the first band to get the crowd really moving on Sunday, no mean feat.'
**Lee Burrows (Praying Mantis Roadie)**

'The band who had played before us had just been bombarded with hundreds of beer cans and I sensed a vibe of fear coming from backstage onlookers… but not from any of us, we were convinced our kind of music was exactly what the kids had paid to hear and we were ready to dish them out the most delicious and hottest brand of heavy metal !!!

**BELOW: The crowd in an ecstatic mood**

'The kids sang their hearts out to every chorus in our repertoire… sheer bliss!! Our jet-lag had worked like some "magic potion" and we nailed every number with all the energy, and charisma which every "end of tour" gig deserves!!! It was one big party… total mayhem broke loose… God Bless `em."
**Marc Storace (Krokus – Vocals)**

'The most memorable thing was the SIZE of the audience. I think there were around 26,000 that year and it felt like we owned the world. Unfortunately, as soon as we hit the stage, a huge beer fight broke out in the audience. There were cans flying in every direction, but happily not too many towards the stage. It was a time when Reading meant

rock festival, and that meant rock bands. Not at all like it is today.'
**Bernie Shaw (Grand Prix – Vocals)**

'One morning, after a heavy downpour, my friend left his tent. He felt something grab his leg, he turned around and there lying deep in mud was this guy in a sleeping bag. He spoke. "What's that up there?" my friend said "What?" "That big orange thing" he replied. "You mean the sun?" There was a pause and then this guy, with a heavy hangover said "yes, it was a tent roof when I went to sleep!" He was so out of it, that during the night somebody pinched his tent from around him without him knowing.'
**Gerald (Jonathan Kelly – Website)**

'It was with great bemusement that the contract for Reading arrived, along with an orange sticker that said something like "Backstage Truck Pass". We were, incidentally, more than happy to see that the fee was £100.00 for the pair of us. So at 10am on the 23rd

we chugged our crappy little rusting Morris Marina (proudly bearing the magic orange sticker) over the backstage grass area to the loading ramp. Four beefy humpers with huge grins jumped down. Two carefully carried my tiny 12-watt one foot square Fender Princeton amp, whilst the other two, not without great dignity, decorum and supreme irony, carefully carried Trimmer's tenor saxophone case onto the stage. So we jumped onstage, went apeshit with screaming sax and guitar pyromaniacs. And, to our astonishment, everybody liked it – insomuch as the 8000-plus crowd cheered and not one beer can was thrown. We even had the whole crowd attempting to win a prize for the best heart attack. A satisfying way to start the day's event, that. Eight thousand folks writhing and a'moaning. We did the business, the four humpers insisted on carefully bringing our two bits of gear back down the ramp, we had a quick chat with a nice couple who ran a band called the Tourists and then got the hell out back

down to SW London for our evening show.'
**Billy Jenkins (Trimmer and Jenkins – Guitar)**

'I remember it being a very aggressive/obnoxious crowd. For some reason they like to pee in bottles and throw them on stage. Thankfully none were thrown at us. I remember getting in Rod McSween's car to leave and some dope crazed lunatic tried to pull my arm off as we sped away. Nice place to play. Apart from that I had a great time.'
**Tommy Aldridge (Pat Travers Band – Drums)**

**LEFT: David Coverdale of Whitesnake – he's a 'Lovehunter'**

**ABOVE: Stocking up on supplies**

'After our appearance I had a drink with Lemmy, whose drink at the time was Special Brew laced with vodka. He offered me a drink and my god I can still taste it to this day!'
**Robb Weir (Tygers of Pan Tang – Guitar)**

'I do remember (since I lived and went to school very near Reading) being in attendance the year that the Hellions were canned off the stage, and Fischer Z got a highly negative reaction. I then sat on the shoulders of my very tall stepbrother Tim so I could fully enjoy the sets of Ian Gillan (right in front of me) and Rory Gallagher (to my right). I was very young.'
**John Wesley Harding (Vocals/Guitar)**

# 1981

**The New Wave of British Heavy Metal (NWOBHM) was now a force to be reckoned with, and favourites like Samson and Lionheart appeared on the bill. The festival also had its first and only 'all female' headline act. There were some 'classic' bands appearing, like The Kinks, Greg Lake and Wishbone Ash, but also the start of something new, with the underground 'second coming' of prog rock, with Twelfth Night opening the festival at 2pm on the Friday afternoon.**

'Our management arranged a pink Cadillac convertible to come pick us up (that apparently once belonged to Jayne Mansfield) with a woman chauffeur, and I remember us being blown all over the place flying along the A4, trying not to get there too late, and we had a minor collision at a roundabout which made us late anyway. Several bikers spotted us en route and "escorted" us the rest of the way in to the site.

"I must have spent most of the day backstage and in the beer tent talking to people, 'cos I don't recall seeing any of the other bands play. Our big neon logo sign laying on the stage behind the drums got smashed by the beer cans being hurled between sound checks. We went onstage and had a really great gig – just remember looking out and seeing a sea of up-for-it people!'
**Kelly Johnson (Girlschool – Vocals/Guitar)**

'There were about 18,000 people there on the Friday and it was a huge landmark for us. It became, seriously, one of the best gigs we ever did. It was absolute magic.'
**Enid Williams (Girlschool – Bass/Vocals)**

'I remember we had the biggest "flash bombs" that they have ever had at Reading; you could hear them five miles away and they nearly blew us up on stage! We are also the only all female band to ever headline Reading Festival.'
**Kim McAuliffe (Girlschool – Vocals/Guitar)**

'I remember there being big screens and they filmed my ass and I got such a huge cheer which was amazing. Then someone threw something at our huge neon sign and it blew up and got smashed to pieces.'
**Denise Dufort (Girlschool – Drums)**

'It was the first time that we had headlined the festival, having built up from early on a Friday, to supporting on a Sunday, to finally headlining on the Saturday. I came back to my house after the show, we were going to have a party, but someone at home told everyone to bugger off, so I came back to an empty house. There was tons of booze around, so I filled my rucksack with a dozen Heinekens from the fridge, got on my motorbike and rode back to the festival site, as I had all the right passes, and just cruised around the campsite for a bit until I found some people who were still awake and had a campfire.

**BELOW: View of the crowd from the stage**

RIGHT: Steve Hackett

'I went up, sat down and said "what did you think of the show?" and we shared the beers around. Looking into the glowing embers of the fire, I saw something move and it was like "shit, what's that? It's a person!!!" So I jumped up to drag them out of the fire and they said "it's alright, he's been there for hours!" Some guy was snuggling up to the embers of the burning fire, he had leathers on so he seemed ok, but his hair and eyebrows had been burnt off! The things people do for rock 'n' roll!'
**Ian Gillan (Gillan – Vocals)**

'We had guitarist Janick Gers by the time we were doing our last Reading appearance, he was watched with interest by Iron Maiden, and was subsequently offered the job with them. They also got their current singer Bruce Dickinson, after seeing him supporting us with Samson.'
**John McCoy (Gillan – Bass)**

BELOW: Off for water

'Greg Lake played with Gary Moore, they did "Fanfare For The Common Man". It was the biggest sound we'd ever heard and we had to follow that. We did, and we had a great time.

'The sun was just going down, we thought that we were going to get an encore; we finished the set to rapturous applause, left the stage and turned around to see all our gear had gone. The Kinks crew had just decided to "whip it off". I think Ray Davies was in a bad mood and had seen enough of us on tour in Europe.'
**Dennis Greaves (Nine Below Zero – Vocals/Guitar)**

'We were back there in 1981 to check out Bruce Dickinson, who was singing with Samson at the time. Things were not working out with Paul Dianno – he seemed to prefer the rock'n'roll lifestyle to the gigs! I went down with Steve Harris because he thought Bruce would be ideal for the band. After they played, Steve thought that Bruce was definitely the one.

'So I approached Bruce in the bar after and asked if we could have a quiet word. We went somewhere quiet in the central backstage area – but probably, being a bit pissed by then, ended out under a light, where everyone in the bar could see us talking animatedly!! Some secret!! Anyway, it worked out, and Bruce joined us soon after.'
**Rod Smallwood (Chairman – Sanctuary Artist Management)**

'It was on this occasion that I decided to try out a new pair of red plastic pants that an ex-girlfriend had put together on a whim. Maybe I should have considered the source. Good thing we weren't playing earlier – these babies were bloody HOT! (Little wonder - plastic doesn't breathe.)
The pants were retired after the show. Perhaps they were burned. At any rate, I never saw them again, nor did anyone else.'
**Billy Squier (Vocals/Guitar)**

'Leaving for the gig, we had a black Granada 2.3 on hire that had been used for the whole tour with a sunroof that had protruding from it a four-foot plastic goose that Bruce had bought in Scotland as a decoy… a decoy for what, we didn't know!
'The gig itself was amazing. I was playing inside my (by then) familiar cage. Prior to us taking the stage, it was covered by

a giant blackout cloth, which made it look like a giant Budgie cage!! The buzz of having that blackout cloth dropped, and being confronted by that amount of lunatics (i.e. the audience) was quite amazing. We had no missiles – Reading tradition – however; I would have been okay anyway, playing inside the cage.

'My theatrical dad showed up, a giant of a man measuring seven foot two, wearing the same mask as myself. He carried Bruce on his shoulders for the encore.'
**Thunderstick (Samson – Drums)**

'We were on about 6 o'clock in the evening, by then we were ready to rock. Not too pissed, but on our way, as you do. Everything went well, until halfway through our set. We went into a ballad with Tony Leach taking lead on piano. By then, Tony was in another world, playing piano, eyes closed, grooving!

**ABOVE: Monday morning and back to work!**

'Someone had a goat and had let it go. The goat decided to stand on Tony's piano, halfway through his solo. Tony opened his eyes and found himself looking at a white goat, standing on his piano, staring at him!

'To see the look on Tony's face was something to behold, my god that smoke was strong!! But he kept playing; this surely was a "fine ole joint".

'We came off to a really fine ovation. Still, it was the goat that made it memorable. At the time, we had a manager who was serving time in prison for fraud. So, that was that, and that is rock 'n' roll.'
**Jackie Lynton (Jackie Lynton's Allstars – Vocals/Guitar)**

# 1982

With American bands in abundance from Twisted Sister, Y&T, Blackfoot and Randy California, to Australian band Cheetah, German headliners MSG and even the Spanish band Baron Rojo, it was 'The United Nations of Metal'. The NWOBHM was also represented by Diamond Head, Rock Goddess, Grand Prix and headliners Iron Maiden. This truly was Reading Rock Festival.

'We had a headlining slot and had just finished recording *Assault Attack* with Graham Bonnet on vocals. We had a show in Sheffield two days before Reading. Graham only lasted 15 minutes on stage in Sheffield and we carried on without vocals for the rest of the show. The question was how to do the Reading headlining gig two days later? So we asked Gary Barden if he would be able to do it at such short notice and he replied with "yes". I remember about 30,000 people waiting to see MSG with Graham Bonnet and when we announced, as we came on stage, that Gary Barden was doing tonight's show, everybody cheered so loud it was almost scary. We had a great show and the people loved it.'
**Michael Schenker (MSG – Guitar)**

'Following the huge success of *The Number of the Beast* we were invited back in 1982 to headline the event. Having

been there so many times and considering the importance of Reading we were very honoured and broke off our US Tour to return from El Paso, play Reading, and then go back to the US to continue touring the next day. The line-up was Bruce, Steve, Davey, Clive and Adrian Smith.'
**Rod Smallwood (Chairman – Sanctuary Artist Management)**

'It was a most incredible rock'n'rollercoaster year, which saw me join the band from being on the dole in March in Aylesbury, to playing a little pub tour of Scotland, to headlining the Marquee more times that I can remember. Playing Reading was an overwhelming thing and sadly a day I can't remember much about. I have some photos of my wife and me, backstage in the sun. One amazing fact is, we were – in '82

**Cheetah, from Australia, get covered in a different kind of 'amber nectar'**

– the only band to have played the festival without a record deal or backing of any kind. That is pretty amazing, but then we had played the Marquee the most times that year I think.'
**Pete Trewavas (Marillion – Bass)**

'This was the biggest gig of Diamond Head's career so far, it was our good fortune to get on the bill because Manowar had pulled out, due to problems obtaining work visas or something, so we were not advertised as playing and we were not on the posters. I remember that our equipment was set up on the left-hand stage while Frank Marino and Mahogany Rush (catchy name) were playing on the right side, and there was no soundcheck other than a quick check to see if our amps were working. I plugged in my Flying V and played a few chords, and a woman came running over and said "do you mind, we are recording a live album." I thought about it and decided "no, fuck off, I am about to play the Reading Festival for the first – and little did I know only time – in front of ten thousand people and it's being recorded for Radio One, why should I care about a bit of spill on your mikes?" So I carried on making sure my amp and guitar were sounding good.

'I heard some Diamond Head fans who had gone back to the camp site, not wanting to see Manowar, were startled to hear the intro to "Am I Evil?" blasting out of the PA, so they came running to get back down the front. The whole gig was broadcast on Radio One's Friday rock show a week or so later, and Sean and I tuned in on a little portable radio. We were both worried about how it would sound, but delighted when it turned out well.'
**Brian Tatler (Diamond Head – Guitar)**

'We co-headlined with Iron Maiden to one of the largest crowds to date. We had played shows together before and they had opened up one of our headline tours in the States, so we had been friends for a while at this point. You could feel the energy from the crowd, and we fed off every ounce of it. It's the type of crowd that makes you surpass your own expectations. At the end of the night, all of us from both bands joined together on stage for a jam. Two drummers, two bass players, multiple guitars and two lead vocalists playing a few random songs, most notably a rendition of "Tush" by ZZ Top. The crowd went into frenzy and you could feel the electricity in the air.'
**Greg T Walker (Blackfoot – Bass/Vocals)**

'My experience was pretty intriguing, on so many levels, never having experienced the English tradition of "bottling and canning" the bands.

There were two stages where the two sides threw the cans and bottles at each other, but they were very creative and very inventive. They would spend hours trapping small pebbles into a litre bottle of Pepsi, just so it would have some 'heft' when it hits the stage, or fill it with piss! So when that started happening it was like "wow! I don't walk" and I was in fight mode. We came into the third song and I was steaming mad, back in the States I would be off the stage every night defending my honour and I was pretty insane back then. People were throwing a lot of stuff and I said "RIGHT ONE AT A TIME, EVERY ONE OF YOU, I WILL MEET YOU AT THE SIDE OF THE STAGE AND I WILL FIGHT EVERY ONE OF YOU!" People started laughing, but I wasn't kidding! I was so fucking angry and they were like "this Yank is fuckin' insane", at that point we won the crowd over. This challenge is documented, I believe, on the Reading album of that year.'
**Dee Snider (Twisted Sister – Vocals)**

'We had played a festival that summer in Wrexham and that was our introduction to England. Motorhead had been on the bill, as they were at the peak of their powers, and Lemmy took us under his wing and when he did that it made it cool to like Twisted Sister. Lemmy looked over us like a protective kind of guy and without him I don't think people would have wanted to take notice of what we were.

'We then recorded our album and were told we were going to do the Reading Festival. I'd known about the Reading Festival as an "Anglophile" record fan for years, so I knew it was popular. We'd already played for 25,000 at an outdoor show in Long Island, so we didn't have a problem playing outdoor shows, but you're in a different country and you're not sure how it's going to go over. I looked on the bill and Blackfoot was on there, Tygers of Pan Tang and Dave Edmunds! I'm a big Dave Edmunds fan, I have all his records from Love Sculpture, so I got all dressed up in make-up, but all I wanted to do was meet Dave Edmunds!

'I knocked on his door and he must have nearly had a heart attack, I was like "MAN its DAVE EDMUNDS" and I was all made up and wearing my six inch boots and he was this little Welshman! I said "I'VE GOT LOVE SCULPTURE, I'VE GOT ALL YOUR SOLO STUFF AND I'VE SEEN ROCKPILE LIKE TEN TIMES!!!" He was just in a state of shock. So he really didn't talk that much.

'I watched some of the other bands and the people throwing shit and I was like "oh boy, this is going to be a rough crowd". So, we walked out during the intro in broad daylight. I don't

drink, but I had a cup, making out it was beer and made a toast and a fucking egg flew right past my head and hit the amp. So, I said to myself "Okay, this is a fucked-up day, so pay attention and watch out for flying items!" We were beating the crowd up and working it, we'd been playing for a long time, so it's a performance technique. We were slowly getting the crowd into it and then, for the big ending, which was "It's Only Rock 'n' Roll But I like It", Lemmy came out with Pete Way and Fast Eddie Clarke and Dee came onstage with a fake machine gun and blasted the crowd, so it was three bass players and three guitarists and it ended great!'
**Jay Jay French (Twisted Sister – Guitar)**

'We met Maiden for the first time and Pete Way had produced our first album, so he went to the show and introduced us to Schenker and I remember there was a lot of drinking going on. There were people that were so drunk, that I didn't know how they were going to go onstage and play! Schenker was completely trashed in the dressing room and I thought "how is he going to play?" But the minute the lights went on onstage he started playing and he was amazing, he looked like someone who hadn't had a drink all day. I was blown away. In those days they were just chucking so much shit up on the stage. It wasn't that bad with us, it was mostly fruit and food. I remember Dave Edmunds was almost up to his knees in apples!'
**Eddie Ojeda (Twisted Sister – Guitar/Vocals)**

'The crowd was insane. It was non stop pandemonium, it was almost riot level, although nobody got hurt and nothing got broken! I don't know if they liked us or hated us. I think we got the largest response of the whole day, we felt like The Beatles walking onstage! I remember that Reading was two different stages and we had the machine gun onstage for "Shoot 'Em Down", not many people expected that.'
**Mark 'The Animal' Mendoza (Twisted Sister – Bass)**

'We had Motorhead jamming with them [Twisted Sister] at the end of the set and Dee ruled the crowd, as he always does.'
**Phil Carson (Atlantic Records)**

'The overall scene was quite different from the festivals this California Boy was accustomed to. The English sky looked dark and threatening. The crowd were all denim and leather, if any females were there please show me proof 'cos believe me I was looking for 'em. This was the height of Heavy Metal.... For this show we were using a hired backline and guitar tech. For the first three songs the guitars were badly out of tune. We kept sending them back to the guy and they kept coming back worse than before. Till finally we just did it ourselves, which only added to the stress I'm sure we were all feeling. Of all the memories of Reading Festival by far the most powerful one is the fans with the beer bottles full of piss and mud having all out war for hours on end. The band was put on notice "If you suck, all those bottles will be coming at you." Not one bottle was thrown at the stage.'
**Phil Kennemore (Y&T – Bass)**

'I was scared stiff. Instead of being the glimmer and flash running around stage left, I was fronting my own very small three piece. I had panicked so much about that, we had a keyboard player to fatten it out. I don't know if he did or not – I couldn't hear him at all on stage. It went really well anyway, it was a lot of fun, the audience were very kind and reactive, they really liked us. That was a far more humbling experience for me than Gillan had ever been!'
**Bernie Torme
(Electric Gypsies – Guitar)**

'I had a new singer, who was from Reading. He practically froze on stage, announcing very quietly between numbers, "I only live down the road".

Micky Moody joined us for two encores, there is an album somewhere of the whole thing. Reading was a gig that all pro musicians wanted to play, it predated almost all of the UK festivals. I know quite a few musicians who never really made the grade professionally that always add the phrase "But I did play the Reading Festival".'
**Bernie Marsden (SOS – Guitar)**

'Guested with Bernie Marsden's SOS in 1982, where I met the Bishop of Reading, who was ligging backstage!'
**Micky Moody (SOS – Guitar)**

# 1983

This year was billed as 'The Last Reading Festival', due to the change in political control in the local council and the site being reclaimed for development. It was the battle of the heavyweights (as depicted on the t-shirt), with Black Sabbath on Saturday and Thin Lizzy on Sunday. This was the only time that Black Sabbath played at Reading, and also the final show in England from Thin Lizzy before they split up. This was also a rare chance to witness Black Sabbath play 'Smoke on the Water', because Ian Gillan was their lead singer for this album and tour.

'I had this beautiful double-wide trailer, with a changing room at one end and a reception at the other for my mum, and all of my cousins and friends, as I was living in Pangbourne at the time. I had this private security firm, two ex-SAS men and Don Arden, the 'FAMOUS' Don Arden, came strolling over and tried to get in to my enclosure (thinking it's the Black Sabbath enclosure) and the guys said "what's your name" and he said "fuck off, I'm the manager of the band!" The guard said "well, your name's not down, sorry." There was steam coming out of his ears; it was a glorious payback moment for all the crap he put me through. We let him in eventually.

'Also, my mother lived across the river in Caversham and I always asked her if she wanted to come along, but she'd always say that she'd skip it as she had people staying. But she changed her mind this year and came out and drove her car to the end of the site where there was a brick wall. She's only about five foot two, so she couldn't see, so she climbed up on her car and still couldn't see, so these bikers, who were sitting on the wall, helped her up. They were a bit curious as to this lady watching a rock show and they eventually dragged it out of her and looked after her very well.'
**Ian Gillan (Black Sabbath – Vocals)**

'Slept in late as I could and relaxed all day, until finally being picked up in the white Rolls Royce with Tony [Iommi] and Geoff [Nicholls] and driving down to the Reading Festival. We played really well and I was well pleased with my own performance. Good crowd response, particularly the encores of "Smoke on the Water" and "Paranoid".
**Bev Bevan (Black Sabbath – Drums)**

'It was kind of bitter sweet: I was born and raised in Reading. It was a great gig and the BBC recorded it and released it. I remember in "Still in Love with You" looking over at Phil and he had tears rolling down his cheek and it was really kind of sad, but it was a very memorable day for that reason. But all things come to an end at some point, and that was our last show in England.'
**John Sykes (Thin Lizzy – Guitar)**

'At the time we had just come back from our first US tour with Andy Ward (ex Camel) on drums, but that had proved a difficult time for Andy. We were second last on, so we had control of the left-hand stage.... We were by now a very different, very sure, organised bunch with a proper road crew, as opposed to the year before. We brought in the more solid rock-style drumming of John Myrter for Reading but Andy was

Possibly the best Finnish band in the world? Michael Monroe of Hanoi Rocks dodges the bottles

**Suzi Quatro – The original
leather clad female rock icon**

there and asked to get up and play as well. We arranged to have two kits, on stage and for the only time ever, featuring two drummers. I remember playing "Grendel"; little did we know it would be for the last time. We were playing well as a band and John's rocky approach was kicking the music along.'
**Pete Trewavas (Marillion – Bass)**

'I seem to remember getting at least one great review (might have been in *Kerrang!)* in which we were praised as the winners of the whole thing and how we had, in a very classy way, made the morons look as dumb as they were. Quite a memorable gig it was. Rock like Fuck.'
**Michael Monroe (Hanoi Rocks – Vocals/Saxophone)**

'The show was a hysterical event; we were late arriving and basically went to the backstage for a toot and beer/spliff and hit the stage running. In front of us was a mass as far as the eye can see of filthy jeans-west wearing long-haired Motorhead/AC/DC t-shirted drunken maniacs.
In the front row I noticed quite a few mascara peroxide-blonde boys w/Hanoi T's on.....hopefully this will be good....

'We started our ruckus, people got into it, good time, no problem... then came the first cheese-burger... the first 40 ounce beer-bottle filled with piss... I thought, no big deal, just a couple of morons venting. That triggered the rest of the morons to vent and the next thing you knew the grey skies of Reading were filled with flying missiles. It turned personal when I saw a grinning idiot in the front row chuck a half-eaten greasy cheese-burger directly at me. I blocked it with my bass, picked it up and walked to the edge of the stage. The poor idiot was wedged in by the people and could not move an inch up or down or sideways, which made him a perfect shiny red-faced target. I took aim... whammo... smack in the middle of the boat. Pieces of onion stuck on the forehead, pieces of mad-cow burger on the eyes and lettuce and ketchup and mayo drippin' down the cheeks and chin.

'I got a massive ovation for my marksmanship and the concert continued. It turned out to be a great gig and we definitely won them over. After the show I had a good piss-up with whoever were on the bill and went to see the headliners, whoever they were. I don't have much recollection.
I do remember that some girl asked to climb on my shoulders to have a better view of whomever it was that was on stage. Me being a skinny runt and drunk as fuck told her that it wasn't a good idea. She wanted to do it anyway. It resulted with her falling face first into a disgusting puddle of mud/piss

and vomit and cursing me to eternal damnation.'
**Sami Yaffa (Hanoi Rocks – Bass)**

'It was an extremely fine day; the band was really on form, it was a great gig and my memory is of 70,000 rockers enjoying an excellent weekend. Suzi Quatro was definitely one of the best acts of the day. I remember telling her so backstage, and she curtsied very demurely and thanked me for saying so…rock bitch…not!!!'
**Robin George (Magnum – Guitar)**

'The Stranglers were still big news at the time and, as Ian Grant was their former manager, plans were afoot to upstage our punk idols. Ian had got in touch with Martin Blake, who was one of the country's leading pyrotechnic experts.

'As we usually finished our set with "Fields of Fire", Martin came up with the idea of setting the band, crew and the entire stage set on fire as part of the finale. He was a bit disappointed when told that only the front part of the stage could be used, and that napalm was still banned in the UK. After he planted his fire bombs of death, he instructed us to be at least eight feet away from them as they were a bit on the warm side (try 30 feet Martin). When the fuckers went off he nearly took out the first ten rows of the audience. The flames shot so high in the air that spotlight operators were seen jumping out of the lighting truss to escape the intense heat. All frontline band members had to be treated for minor burns and our publicist Alan Edwards refused to let anyone photograph us for a month. For the next few weeks the people of Reading were walking around with no fucking eyebrows.'
**Bruce Watson (Big Country – Guitar)**

'It was the first big concert my one-year-old daughter attended, she was running around backstage grooving to all the bands, in fact, via the intercom in our house, the first words out of Laura's mouth were "ROCK AND ROLL"...believe it or not! I had a good band then, as always, with two backing singers who were sisters. One of them had had her hair done in braids, a la the Caribbean, she's white, so it was slightly unusual and she sang especially soulful that night. Wonder if the hair had anything to do with it? 'We had wonderful reviews. They said I was the big "surprise" hit of the festival.'
**Suzi Quatro (Singer/Bass)**

'We went on in a slot two before Thin Lizzy, who were headlining. Reading was still quite mainstream then. No disposable pop, but plenty of melody, if you take my point.

It was, even as recently as '83, like taking your life into your own greasy hands, just popping out for a piss. Any thoughts of "number twos", well, don't even think about going down that cul-de-sac. Stay in your hotel room until the last possible moment, that was the best advice.'
**Steve Harley (Steve Harley and the Cockney Rebel – Vocals/Guitar)**

'I was 14 and that was the year Thin Lizzy headlined, when Reading really was rock! I've since found out that was their last UK performance. My dad took me and my brother for the weekend. My dad was a pal of Phil Lynott and I got to meet the band and sat in Scott Gorham's portakabin where all their guitars were, trembling with excitement while he warmed up. I couldn't believe how many guitars they had. I remember sitting low in our seats in the car outside the site on an industrial estate up that long road with our kid smoking joints, one eye on two cops havin' a brew at a fry-up van, feeling pretty damn grown up and outlawish! Also witnessing that strange phenomenon of kids making campfires with two-litre plastic beer bottles. It fucking reeked. Great weekend.'
**Jimi Goodwin (Doves – Vocals/Bass/Guitar/Drums)**

'The band's highly successful Reading debut nearly didn't take place at all. This was due to the band's previously faithful tour coach "Vic" literally grinding to a halt on the M6 on the way to the festival, leaving the band, crew and gear stranded on the hard shoulder, in the middle of nowhere.

'We eventually arrived at the festival site early on Friday morning, thinking that was the end of the mishaps. However, more panics were to follow later on in the day when the band got stranded on a non-moving train, only returning to the site

ABOVE: Pat McManus of Mama's Boys

five minutes before the deadline. Then, during the set, Niall's amplifier, hired for the occasion, decided to pack up during "Crown of Thorns". Fortunately, the problems didn't destroy the set and by the closing number the crowd had been well and truly won over. As the chorus of "Atlantis" reached its stunning climax, with the Olympic torch blazing in the hands of Euan, the crowd's roar of approval set the seal on the most momentous day of the band's career so far.'
**Mike Bentley (Pallas Fanzine Editor)**

'We reformed to play the 25th anniversary of the Marquee Club and added six more dates, including the Reading Festival. Radio One recorded our set and it was later released on the Strange Fruit label. Thanks to Woodstock the music business had changed a lot. It was more commercial. Record labels had their hospitality marquees backstage.
One journalist, who shall remain nameless, asked what numbers we'd played in our set. He was there to write a review but had not managed to leave the beer tent. It was a different vibe from what I remembered of the earlier festivals. In the artistes' car park someone, in an attempt to steal the wheels off my Jeep, had loosed the studs. On the way to the airport the next day a wheel came adrift on the M40. It was a narrow escape. Whatever happened to peace and love?'
**Leo Lyons (Ten Years After – Bass)**

'In fact it was a great experience to play at the Reading Festival, to be along with such acts as Stevie Ray Vaughan, Black Sabbath etc. Especially as we were so young, and only the year before had been playing in the wilds of Ireland.'
**Pat McManus (Mama's Boys – Vocals/Guitar/Fiddle)**

# 1984 & 1985

In 1984, due to the closure of the site at Reading the previous year, the ill-fated 'Reading Rocks On' was attempted. This was to be the 24th NJF Festival and was to be held in Lilford, Northamptonshire. The line-up featured classic rock in the form of Jethro Tull, Hawkwind and Nazareth, and an odd mixture of support acts. This would have probably sealed the fate of Hanoi Rocks and Phil Lynott's Grand Slam as major league contenders, but it wasn't meant to be and the show was cancelled – less than a week before it was due to be held – when the council refused the licence. This would also have been the first festival headline performance for Marillion.

'I went to the festival in 1984, it was a very lonely day,
and there wasn't anybody there!!'
**Harry James (Terraplane – Drums)**

# 1986

**The festival was back, due to a change in the Reading Council. The Labour Party were back in after an election victory and one of their promises was to allow the festival to be held again. Though slightly further down Richfield Avenue, in an adjacent field to the previous site, it was business as usual.**

**Dumpy and his 'dancer' performing on stage**

'There were a lot more 'indie' bands than usual in the mix, Lords Of The New Church, the Bolshoi, the Mission and New Model Army, all rubbing shoulders with the usual rock bands including Hawkwind, Rough Cutt, FM, the Enid and Saturday night headliners Saxon.

'I think this was the last of the "old school" Readings, before it went a little more current and contemporary. I think we played on the Friday afternoon and Killing Joke were headlining....

'It was raining fairly heavily and backstage was just a mud bath. For the artistes' comfort, some planks of wood were laid down as a walkway in the mud, so we could walk from dressing room to stage to toilet to backstage bar without getting our precious little tootsies too dirty and wet. However, it was still fairly slippery out there and one of the unfortunates

of the day was the guitarist, I think, from Twenty Flight Rockers. He was tiptoeing his way along one of these planks on his way to the stage, adorned in his finest new, shiny leather pants, jacket and boots when he slipped and went head first into the mud. We were watching from the window of our backstage caravan, and whilst cackles of laughter were heard all throughout the backstage area, the guy just got up covered in mud and went on stage. What a trooper....

All the reviews I've ever read or reports I've ever heard about our performance that afternoon suggest that I fell off the front of the stage. Not true. As inebriated as I was, I have a very clear recollection of standing at the edge of the stage, looking down, and deciding to jump. It was a very conscious decision to leap. It may have looked like a fall, and it certainly was a little foolish as I think it was at least 15 feet down, but I landed on my feet and I didn't lose my hat. But it did hurt a little.'

**Wayne Hussey**
**(The Mission – Vocals/Guitar)**

'Both years I rode my bike onto the stage, the stage manager made me empty the fuel tank and I had to ride on with only a carburettor's worth of fuel. I was more nervous about this than playing in front of my largest crowd ever, because the thing was that if the fuel had of run out half way up the ramp, I could have easily fallen off and of course blown my chance of playing.

'As I had toured with Hawkwind in '85, I was already well-known by their followers, so to be asked to go on stage with Lemmy and sing backup vocals on "Silver Machine" and be well-received was a great experience, plus I thoroughly enjoyed myself.'

**Dumpy (Dumpy's Rusty Nuts – Vocals/Guitar)**

'We always had a great following and through our fan club we were told that a lot of the fan base would be camping in the

same area, so I decided I would camp out for the weekend. I remember a band who we knew called Engine had come to the camp site with their Transit and all their equipment plus a generator, so on the Saturday night we had a camp site gig and it was real good fun.

'We played on the Saturday afternoon and I remember as we went on stage Dumpy roaring up the entrance ramp on his Triumph motorbike; that certainly got the fans going. We played a great set, and I remember Lemmy being to my stage left for most of the set. Saxon headlined the Saturday night that year, backstage there was a big hole dug and a fence put round it, and we wondered what all the fuss was about. I asked Brian Pithers, who was the local radio rock DJ what the hole was for. He replied "It's pyrotechnics for the end of Saxon's set." Unfortunately it rained extensively that evening and instead of a huge bang there was just a sort of a puff and a movement within the water that had gathered in the hole, so I suppose you could say that you can't beat heavy metal or a heavy downfall!'
**Mick Kirton (Dumpy's Rusty Nuts – Drums)**

'The Labour Party in Reading fought and won elections on a commitment to try and bring the festival back to the town. So in May 1986, after just two year's experience as a councillor, I found myself charged with the job of

persuading the then promoter, Harold Pendleton, that Reading Festival would be safe now that Labour was running the council.

'I tracked Harold down to the Marquee Club in Soho, which he still owned, and a number of interesting meetings soon followed. Harold had attempted to re-create the Reading Festival at venues in Spain and Milton Keynes, both of which were disasters. If he was to be persuaded to return to Reading, he needed to know that the council would not pull the plug by requiring either a licence or the use of the Thameside Promenade.

**Ruby Turner brings some soul to the stage**

'It was a make-or-break decision, because after a two-year absence in 1984 and 1985 it would be almost impossible to re-establish Reading in the festival calendar if we missed out again in the summer of 1986. For the festival to break even financially it had to attract around 30,000 fans. The hurriedly-arranged 1986 festival attracted only 17,000 – hardly surprising, given that Hawkwind were one of the main attractions! Nevertheless, both Harold and the council kept faith in the festival and within two years the crowds were back and Reading was rocking again.
**Martin Salter (Labour MP Reading West)**

'One summer I took a longboat with my family and chugged up the Thames. We came across a Reading Festival in progress, so I moored the barge to a grassy bank and dragged my two sons then aged 6 and 12 and the wife across the muddy field and gatecrashed backstage. Well, the promoters knew me! I got talking with some new band I'd never heard of while my kids got passes to see the

show out front. Suddenly my 12-year-old comes running back crying. He'd been struck by a coke can and a flying water bottle. Apparently the band on stage weren't going down too well and my son got the wrath of the audience's vengeance.'
**Keith Emerson (The Nice/ELP – Keyboards)**

'What was really great was when we were done playing we went out into the crowd to buy some drinks and a bunch of the guys who were throwing shit at us and flipping us off bought us beers! We couldn't believe it! They were totally cool and we ended up partying with them all night! Reading is definitely way more CRAZY than any other festivals I've ever played! Everybody there gets trashed and becomes really rowdy!'
**Amir Derakh (Rough Cutt – Guitar/Keyboards)**

'The event seemed to have lost its lustre and it was just another gig, although I think the set my four-piece band delivered was pretty strong and we went down well.'
**Graham Parker (Vocals/Guitar)**

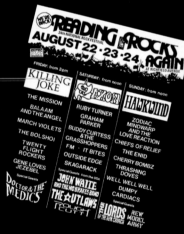

**Dr and the Medics**

'I don't remember Reading. I hate festivals!!!!!!'
**Frank Dunnery (It Bites – Vocals/Guitar)**

'I remembered looking out at the crowd and thought, "they are not going to go for this, we play soul music and they look like hardcore heavy metal fans." Still, that was not going to put me off, I'm here to stay and sing I will! I had a new keyboard player with me that day. His first gig with me. So he was a little nervous, I guess, but we reassured him he'd be fine. We gave it some stick as they say in Birmingham, ducking the odd clump of sodden earth that came our way. Then,

**Martin Salter, Labour MP for Reading West**

from somewhere deep in the crowds of faces, came a bottle of what could only be urine, it couldn't have been "good ole cider", they needed that! It came whistling over the heads of the crowd in the front and landed a direct hit on the new keyboard player's piano. He freaked and we laughed. What else could we do? We were in the middle of the set and there was no escape but to carry on and finish the gig. We got through and despite the fizzy urine bottle incident we loved it! If only to say we were there, it was good enough, and looking back it most certainly was.'
**Ruby Turner (Ruby Turner – Vocals)**

# 1987

**With a more rock-orientated line-up, this was probably the last 'real' Reading Rock Festival. With classic rock headliners Alice Cooper and Status Quo, supported by new rockers the Quireboys, Lizzy Borden, Kooga, Virginia Wolf and Vow Wow, the festival again looked healthy. There was also an abundance of 'new' indie bands, the Babysitters, the Godfathers, All About Eve and the first festival headline appearance for the Goth band the Mission. All was good in Berkshire and the festival was back on top.**

'There was never anything thrown on stage, it was really amazing. I said our show is a little bit different, when we are doing our job, they are going to be so interested in the show that they won't have time to throw anything and that is exactly what happened. I think that if you get up on stage and you are just up there jamming, the audience is going to get restless and they're going to do what they do. If you keep the audience so riveted to what you're doing, visually and musically at the same time, they honestly don't want to look away, as they are going to miss something!! That's why we never have any violence in our audience. That's our secret weapon!! When we got there it was pouring rain and it was a mudfest. Outdoor festivals and rain just go together.'
**Alice Cooper (Alice Cooper – Vocals)**

'I remember standing there and Bad News was on; there was an amount of bottles and shit that was flying through the air. Lemmy was standing beside me and he said "we started this" and he was really proud of the fact! People were getting hit with bottles; for a while that festival was one to stay clear of, but I've heard that now it's quite a good festival to go to again.'
**Francis Rossi (Status Quo – Vocals/Guitar)**

'We were on a Saturday night, with our own tent with champagne and Lemmy was in their "necking it" as ours was the fun tent, it was a free drink tent!!! That was when Lenny Henry was rude to Bob's mum.'
**Mark Stanway (Magnum – Keyboards)**

'We were on before Alice Cooper. The two main stages were side by side. During our set I could hear a snare drum being hit constantly. This went far beyond a mere soundcheck. And besides, how dare whoever it was do it while we were on stage? Every time we ended a song I could hear this infernal snare drum being hit. Old show biz tricks like this, to fuck up the support basically, I'd already encountered and did not tolerate. Besides, it's fucking rude.

'We were recording the gig for what would eventually become

*All Live and All of the Night*. My hackles were up and I remember screaming out to Max Bisgrove, our sound man to "make their ears bleed, Max" just before the guitar solo in "London Lady". After we got off stage I went round to Alice Cooper's stage to find their tour manager. It took three Hell's Angels to drag me off the wanker.'
**JJ Burnel (The Stranglers – Bass)**

'Cobalt crashed out the first chords and we ran onto the stage, the first thing that hit me was a dead rabbit full in the face and then I saw the piss bottles. Dozens of them spinning out of the sun and exploding all over the stage. How we got through the set I'll never know. And then at the end of the last number, it happened. The sublime, the amazing, the transcendental, the piss Christ incident. I remember it clearly, like a vision. The adrenaline kicked in, that fight or flight chemical that turns the world into slow motion. I gazed into the setting sun and saw this two-litre plastic Evian bottle filled with yellow piss come slowly somersaulting in, it was so slow I could almost count the revolutions it made as it rolled out of the sky.

'I followed its trailing image as it passed over Cobalt's head, the Stargazer noticed it too, his hands fell from his guitar and his mouth dropped slowly open. The music slurred down from 45 to 33, Slammy threw off a perfect drum roll and finished with a tight snare flamm, he jumped up in ultra slo-mo, reached out his right hand and grabbed the revolving bottle clean out of the sky, the piss exploded, drenching the drummer from head to toe. The divine drummer boy threw his arms out in a crucifix position, bottle in one hand, sticks in the other, grinning beatifically, holy glow backlights making him shine in the piss like Jesus himself. The crowd screamed hosannas for the man! Piss Christ baby! Fuck yeah!
I tell you star child, it was one fucking way to end a gig.
I mean, come on man, it's not every band that has God working the special effects.'
**Zodiac Mindwarp (Zodiac Mindwarp & The Love Reaction – Vocals)**

Alice Cooper's only appearance at Reading

Wayne Hussey of the Mission commands the 'Goth contingent'

When Alice Cooper played Reading he was pissed off because his snake wasn't sent any accreditation (backstage pass, sticker for the car, guest passes etc). We were told that Alice had arrived with the band half an hour before, but that a dude in a suit was at the backstage gate in a limo claiming to be the artiste.

'On investigating, it was Alice, dressed like an accountant in a three-piece suit and tie, complete with briefcase, hair scraped back, ponytail hidden and no make-up. When I stuck my head in the car he said, "If you'd sent (name of snake escapes me) his? (her?) passes, I wouldn't have had to give mine away and this wouldn't have been necessary." The snake got its passes.'
**Paul Kale (Guest List Organiser)**

'Possibly the first big festival we played. We came on at sunset. I had no idea that we would do as well as we did. Rick Price yells "we're in goddamn England!" and the set just took off. A few years later, we were playing at the Town and Country and a geezer comes up with a t-shirt and says (in an incredibly thick, god knows from what part of your island, accent) "Sign 'er up mate. Saw yas at Reading. I was there, inna mud! Bastard genius!" I don't think I've ever been given a compliment I believed anymore than the one that guy gave us.'
**Dan Baird (The Georgia Satellites – Vocals/Guitarist)**

'The first time I had ever drunk Jack D and Coke. I was in the backstage bar and Lemmy asked me what I was drinking. I answered "lager", so he then said try this, and handed me a pint glass of what I thought was Guinness. And WOW, I had my very first taste of JD and Coke... and now that's history!

'Sometime after playing my set I was in the backstage bogs standing next to a singer from one of the bands who had followed me. Now, for legal reasons I'm not going to say who it was, but anyway he said to me in a somewhat rather West Midlands dialect: "Dumpy, did you see what happened to me? We were getting so many plastic bottles thrown at us I thought I'd be a bit flash so I picked one up and took a drink from it." Now, we all know what's on those plastic bottles, don't we? He didn't!!!'
**Dumpy (Dumpy's Rusty Nuts – Vocals/Guitar)**

'I found out later from a local that the audience throws things when they like you. They also throw things when they don't like you. It's all a bit confusing to me....'
**Lee Aaron (Lee Aaron – Vocals)**

**Lee Aaron flys the flag for Canada**

'That year Paul Samson guested on guitar with us for a couple of songs and there was a notable performance by the band Bad News. I remember standing at the bottom of the exit ramp when the band came off stage. I jokingly said to Spider the drummer "That was terrible", and he replied with a big cheesy grin "Yes, and that's the best I've ever played!" Still, they did have Brian May playing with them, so they must have been doing something right.'
**Mick Kirton (Dumpy's Rusty Nuts – Drums)**

'You also tend to remember, even though you wish you didn't, being drunk. In my case it involved staggering around shouting that I didn't like Alice Cooper. It says much for the other festival goers that they didn't punch me. Actually, Alice Cooper was great and the stage show involving execution and decapitation was enjoyably convincing. Nice one Alice.'
**Bev Rogers
(Gardener and Horticulturist)**

'I think I don't have time, sadly ... and remembering this is not the easiest either! Maybe Ade Edmondson ought to write it!'
**Brian May (Queen/
Bad News – Guitar)**

**Bad News prepare backstage, for the onstage 'bottling'**

'Unfortunately the first night was marred by someone breaking into my tent, which I shared with my brother, and taking both our sleeping bags plus five cans of beer (they left us one!!). All three nights were spent wrapped up in our friend's car seat covers (which kind of kept the cold air at bay). But the music made up for it – Status Quo/Alice Cooper and the band I really went for – The Georgia Satellites.'
**Andy 'Harry the Bannister' Harris (MOD Employee)**

# 1988

It all went terribly wrong in 1988. From the bottling of Bonnie Tyler, Deacon Blue and Meat Loaf, to the poor supporting line up – Bonfire, John Hiatt and the Hothouse Flowers – the festival was at an end in its existing form. Something had to be done and soon. With a poor Saturday night headliner in Starship, which no longer included Grace Slick (who had seen the error of her ways and left) to the session tent which featured bands who amounted to nothing, the festival was doomed and this would be the end for the NJF-run festival.

'I think the posters still said "Reading Rock & Blues Festival". I remember it was the only time that we played with our original bass player in the band and Bob used to prowl in front of the monitors, with his "busted-up" teeth growling at the audience. I wore the black t-shirt with all the Acid House "smiley faces" as a piss take. It was the "Summer Of Love" and it was all just kicking off. It may even have been our first festival and it was back when they had the split stages. I think that Fields of the Nephilim were on before us. My brother always said that they were a duo, because you could only ever see two members of the band at a time, due to the smoke!'
**Miles Hunt (The Wonderstuff – Vocals/Guitar)**

'My memory of Reading Festival, the first time around, was lowly on the bill with a guarantee off £300.00 plus VAT, I believe. But unfortunately the cheque bounced on us, so we never got paid that.'
**Les Johnson (The Wonderstuff Tour Manager)**

'On arrival we heard tales of Meat Loaf being bottled off the stage the day before – I think we were the first act on. We were going down pretty well and the crowd built solidly during the show I was doing with Ronnie. To close our show we had this number called "Down the Road" that contained bizarre impressions – for instance, we did Boris Becker and

Iggy Pop in the spotlights

78

batted the microphone across the stage with the back of the guitar. To finish off the song, I had primed the stage crew with bottles and sang "I want to hear Meat Loaf down the road". At this point the roadies started hurling missiles at the two of us. The audience picked up on the gag immediately and were delighted to join in. It was bloody scary but very funny. We left the stage with the crowd cheering and headed for the bar.

'A delighted Jack Barry presented us with a bottle of champagne; we were very pleased with ourselves and continued to get legless very quickly. It seemed like I had started a trend, as a couple of the next acts suffered from the joke I had set up and had to curtail their sets. I heard that Jack Barry was now looking for us to go back on and do a couple more numbers and was searching for us with an envelope containing a couple of grand, should I wish to help fill a gap that was appearing in the afternoon's show. Sadly I was drunk and my girlfriend Karen whisked me away from Reading, which probably was the most sensible thing to do in the circumstances.'
**John Otway (Vocals)**

'I believe that we [Meat Loaf] didn't play a full set that day because of what happened.'
**Bob Kulick (Meat Loaf – Guitar)**

'I was back in New York, and read it on a new stand that sold foreign music papers. The cover of the UK-based *Melody Maker* read: "The Public Humiliation of Meat Loaf."

'This had been one of the strangest shows of my career, and I've played a whole lot of shows over the past 40 years. I had been a member of the Meat Loaf band for several years in the late eighties, when we played the Reading Festival. When the band played the UK we had generally been treated with reverence, like rock 'n' roll royalty. When we got to the Reading Festival, Bonnie Tyler was on stage, and nearly done with her set. I stood at the side of the stage and saw she was having a bit of trouble with some of the crowd who were obviously drunk, and hurling things at her and the band. Bonnie was a trooper and got through it, in spite of the rowdy crowd. I took a few hits off of a Heineken beer, and then checked the tuning of my guitar. When we hit the stage we started off with the song "Out of the Frying Pan". The first thing I noticed, apart from the vast sea of thousands of people in the crowd, were the ninja type silver circles flying up at us at high speeds. On closer inspection it was clear that these were flattened beer tins. They make for a very menacing presence, and not

conducive for concentrating on playing music. I was dodging these objects, as were the others in the band, and hoping one wouldn't hit me.

'It would get more bizarre. When we started our second number I saw large plastic soda bottles were coming up at the stage and they were spinning fast, and spilling out liquid. They hit one of the backing singers, after soaking both of them with the contents of the bottle. It was only after contact that the girls came back to me and informed me that it was urine in the bottles. After the first song Meat Loaf was furious and verbally chastised the crowd, saying that he would stop performing if people didn't stop hurling things at the stage.

'We left the stage after only two numbers. Then we got back on stage. We had to, as a majority of the audience were loudly demanding more. However, this time the objects, the aforementioned bottles and flattened tins, came faster and more furiously at us. Meat Loaf spotted one of the culprits, a ringleader, and actually jumped off stage and started beating one of them up. Then another, then another. He had pummelled three of the offenders into submission. I thought I was dreaming. All the while we're vamping on a chord, taking solos, filling time, while our fearless leader was beating up the audience. I couldn't believe what I was seeing.

'Meat Loaf made a throat-slicing finger motion at the band for us to cut it short, and it was over. We left the stage, got into the bus, then back to the London White House Hotel. I went straight to the bar for a vodka rocks and after a few sips I thought, what a strange day that was!'
**Alan Merrill (Meat Loaf – Guitar)**

'Before we went, on I got the announcer to say that Mick Box has requested that nobody should throw any bottles onto the stage, but bring them to the side of the stage and after his performance he would drink them. It seemed to work, as we had very little thrown at us.'
**Mick Box (Uriah Heep – Guitar)**

'We used to run the Reading Festival, because we were the Marquee Club and my boss Jack Barrie used to book the bands there. The Quireboys were one of the bands that I liked, so I put them on at the festival and they said they wanted to travel down in style. So the whole fee was spent on a limousine and a Bentley (which was owned by a mate of mine), but they wanted to stay in a hotel as well. Keith Allen was very well-known and he was hanging out the back of

the car all the way down the M4, filming them throwing beer bottles out the window of the car. We got down to Reading and we had to stop at the off licence, before we actually go to the festival, then we went to the hotel, checked in. Then Ginger got arrested, so we were without a guitar player, he'd knocked a policeman's hat off! And that was before the gig! He had one phone call and he called Spike in the hotel and he said "I've been arrested, what can I do?" Spike said "I don't know?" and put the phone down. But they did let him out and it was a cracking gig! That was close to when I stopped managing them, to be honest!!'
**Bush Telford (Marquee Club Manager)**

'It was the first time that I met Alice Cooper.... I remember the night Meatloaf played and he was hit by a green apple, right in the nose. He kept going off and then coming back on, because if he didn't play the minimum amount of time, he wouldn't have got paid!'
**Spike (The Quireboys – Vocals)**

'The thing about backstage in these places is that they kept changing the dressing rooms around and we may not have even stayed for the headliners.'
**Nigel Mogg (The Quireboys – Bass)**

'I heard a rumour that Meat Loaf was hit in the head with a two-litre plastic bottle filled with urine and left the stage after three songs. Once I heard that, I was more prepared for this type of audience. As expected, someone threw a two-litre bottle of piss on stage and unbeknownst to them, this Yank played soccer, or as you say football, in my youth. I flipped the bottle up behind me while I was still playing guitar and kicked the bottle back into the crowd and
it spun around, spraying at least 30 people. It was amazing. The bottle was twirling around like a helicopter's propeller.
That was the last bottle anyone threw on stage at us.'
**Jim Babjack (The Smithereens – Guitar)**

**A very relaxed afternoon**

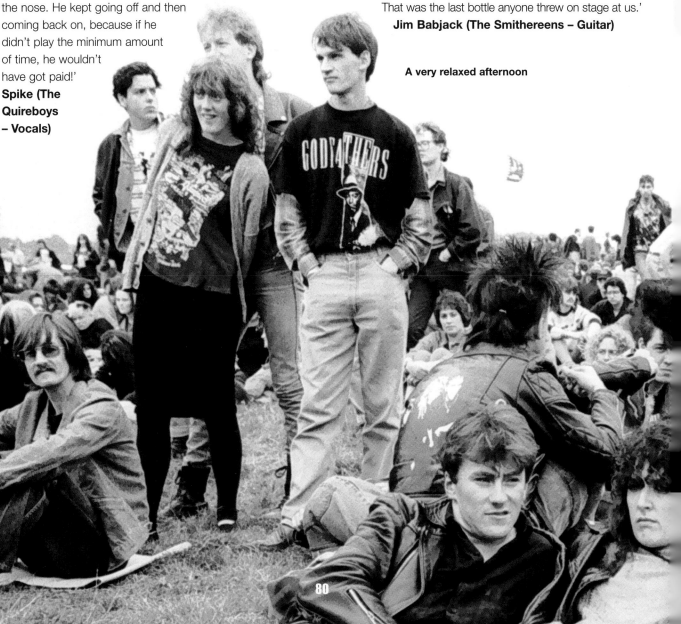

Starship fly into the headline slot

# 1989

**Like a phoenix from the flames, this was the year that the Reading Festival was re-born. With the involvement of the Mean Fiddler organisation and an improved line-up, the festival was no longer Reading Rock, but a new 'indie hybrid', and a festival that would prove to be more durable and popular than ever.**

'Again, I have very little recollection of the day apart from meeting Roger Whittaker in our backstage caravan before the show. Apparently, his son was a huge Mission fan. The only other memory I have is of downright sleazy, decadent, and sordid goings-on back at the local hotel that night. I won't go into details, but suffice to say that I had two rooms that night and was going back and forth between the two all night.'
**Wayne Hussey (The Mission – Vocals/Guitar)**

'To me, muddy fields are the domain of sheep and cattle, not human beings. Give me a nice comfy theatre or arena anytime!'
**Philip Chevron (The Pogues – Guitar)**

'There was a certain sense of achievement in being invited to play at one of the world's most famous rock festivals, although this was slightly tempered by the fact that most people thought we'd been placed on the wrong day and didn't fit in with the bands that surrounded us! We didn't care, though. We took the stage and launched into "Kennedy". During this period we used to indulge in slightly ridiculous stage antics… lots of running around, lying on our backs waggling our feet in the air, forward rolls and stuff. I can't remember how the crowd reacted to our appearance but since most of them wouldn't have had a clue who we were I imagine it wasn't totally ecstatic and I've probably erased it from my memory!'
**David Gedge (The Wedding Present – Vocals/Guitar)**

'I do remember the photo op after our performance. A gaggle of shutterbugs were gathered before us with the usual elbows and knees warfare. In the back of the pack, I noticed an exposed bellybutton with its owner up on tiptoes, trying to get a decent shot. I cried out for the fellas to let the lady come forward, if indeed this was still a country of gentlemen. The pissed and polluted sea parted, and I finally got a look at bellybutton's face as she determinedly made her way to the front. She was a stunner: a blue eyed Andalucian with a wicked Tuareg streak. I gave her a wink and she smiled back. Shit, game over. A few bent spoons later, I saw her in the hospitality tent and asked if I could take her out to dinner sometime. She agreed, as long as I promised to take a bath beforehand. A couple months later, I took that bath and went out on the longest date of my life. We've been married 15 years and I still fear for my soul when I see that smile.'
**Dan Stuart (Green On Red – Vocals/Guitar)**

'I seem to remember we all stayed up rather late the night before, which made us late getting to Reading. We were still outside waiting to get in 15 minutes into the time we were meant to play. Finally, worse for wear, we plugged straight into our amps to open the festival for that day… we were the worse for partying. I drank too much and took too much acid. I woke up in a local hedgerow the next day.'
**Robber de Offlicence  (Gaye Bykers On Acid – Bass)**

'We were scheduled to be the first band on the main stage. I had arrived early, separately from the band, and we were due to set our gear up two hours or so before we were due to play. One hour before showtime and the other members of the band who were travelling with the gear had still not arrived on site. I had no idea where they were. Bear in mind this was in the days before mobile phones. The stage manager was a big ruddy-faced bald fella whose name I can't recall. He was calling me and my band all the names under the sun, threatening to pull us from the gig. Luckily they arrived just before the stage manager's deadline and the crew hastily set up the gear in front of a rapidly swelling audience. With the help of the crew, we hit the stage at the appointed hour. The new era of Reading had kicked off amid mild pandemonium. We had no sound check to speak of and suffice to say we rocked the house. I think!!'
**Mary Byker (Gaye Bykers On Acid – Vocals)**

'I went all the way to the very back of the crowd, miles from the stage. The Sugarcubes were announced and looked like little dolls walking on stage, which convinced me even further that this outdoor business was no way to see a band. I loved their music but had never seen them live. Then Bjork started singing. She was only a speck on stage but her voice absolutely boomed all the way back to me and seemed to shoot above us into the air. I could not believe this sonic blast was coming from such a little thing so far away!

'Thousands of people were there but you could have heard a pin drop. I kind of got that this was more than just getting pissed and muddy to a live soundtrack. The elements and all the strangers around you were kind of the point. The backstage scene that weekend was also one of my favorite band memories of all time. I was living with Steve [from That Petrol Emotion] at the time and happily both our bands were on the bill. It was a great time for us because everyone's band seemed to be doing well. All our friends seemed to have deals or be getting radio play and it seemed like everyone was invited to play at Reading that year. I remember quietly stopping that day and telling myself how lucky I was to be there, at that time, with all those bands that I really loved.

'Unfortunately, without realizing it at first, it was also starting to make me incredibly nervous. I couldn't relax and have fun. I couldn't properly smile or dance or even sing well. I was kind of just locked into this terror. So, in reality, the show itself, as far as the performance goes, was a nightmare.'
**Tracey Belland (Voice of the Beehive – Vocals/Guitar)**

**RIGHT: Miles Hunt of the Wonderstuff**

**BELOW: Are you in the crowd? Answers on a postcard**

'Just as we were about to start, the rain cleared up and a beautiful rainbow appeared in the sky. The crowd was full of love, and was the biggest we had ever played for. We were horribly out of tune, but the audience didn't seem to mind. I did, though, and took to throwing my guitar up into the air as high as I could, over and over.'
**Paul Leary (The Butthole Surfers – Guitar)**

'All I hear is that there are other people, who say the same thing as me, that they can't remember being there. Someone from 10cc, who were headlining, can't remember being there. So I have added my name…"Hank Wangford can't remember being there". It's not that I was so drug ravished

or anything, I think that it was just a supremely ordinary festival that was completely unmemorable. Or else it was just in another dimension. There is something otherworldly about the fact that there are now three of us that think the Reading Festival didn't exist, it was only in people's imagination.'
**Hank Wangford (Hank Wangford Band – Vocals/Guitar)**

'We had Iggy Pop's sound man (we had just finished the European tour for the *Instinct* album as his support group). We were at the top of our game and sounded huge, the crowd went mad. Kev Reverb punched the stage manager after the gig 'cos he was moaning about something we had done on stage (throwing microphones into the crowd probably).

'Elvis Costello and Shane McGowan from the Pogues spent the WHOLE festival in the bar that year... livers must have been hanging out their asses by the end. Pop Will Eat Itself did their best to ignore us I remember... snooty fuckers....? I copped off with two American go-go dancers... that's about all I remember....'
**Porkbeast (Crazyhead – Bass)**

'I barely got to the festival in time, as there were colossal traffic jams on the way down of the type which necessitated nipping out of the car and over an embankment for a piss. Given I was in my stage clothes, as the lines between stage and street have always been somewhat blurred for me, staggering up a grassy hill and clambering over a fence whilst wearing tight black clothes, enough eyeliner to make Amy Winehouse look

like an amateur, half a ton of chunky silver Goth jewellery, huge hair and enormous boots drew a pre-festival round of applause from the rest of the jam.

'After I breathlessly took the stage in the nick of time, the gig went fine, if I remember correctly. It was the usual hilarious festival banter and the recitation of some of my throat-cuttingly dark poetry, a roller-coaster combination that usually does the trick. I then repaired to the Payments Office, which was a small caravan, where I was paid in cash – somewhat unusual – but it was only the acoustic area and well, festivals, eh? Crazy, man.

'I trotted off gleefully. clutching my paltry wad of limp fivers to meet New Model Army, also on the bill that year alongside the Pogues. After a blinding gig by NMA, I waded through the usual tedious festival backstage flotsam of leathery blonde groupies, wizened cokeheads and weasley music hacks, all trying to look cool and failing miserably, and surprised the Army's then manager sitting in their dressing room – another caravan – white as a sheet and shaking visibly. "What's the matter", I cried. He looked at me with a mixture of horror and awe on his face. "They paid me in cash", he hissed. "Cash! All of it! Thousands and thousands of pounds in used tenners, it's all gaffered to my body, under me vest! I can't go anywhere, not even the bog – I've never known the like. You used to be a bouncer; you'll have to be my bodyguard!"

'Which is why New Model Army's manager was accompanied everywhere he went at that Festival – and I mean everywhere – by a tall, black-clad Goth woman looking like a member of the Alternative SAS Covert Festivals Cadre and visibly trying not to giggle hysterically whilst pretending hilariously to talk into an invisible headset – bogs are clear, repeat, bogs are clear, we are go on bogs, Red Leader, over and out.'
**Joolz (Spoken Word/Poet)**

'I made my way to the main stage to supervise the set-up, prior to the band's arrival. Something which did eventually happen, just in time. Actually, my input was rather minimal (I'm not sure whether that was down to my limited knowledge or the backstage crew's professionalism – I suspect the latter). I vividly remember this small girl, during a brief shower, approached me for a light, dressed in little more than a bikini/skirt outfit.

'Following Spaceman's performance, the rest of the day was up for grabs. By the evening I had somehow found my way onto the photographers' platform to the right of the main stage. And, there, on stage, was that girl again – apparently her name was Bjork.'
**Henri Hood (Spacemen 3 – tour manager)**

'My strongest memory is that although we were 35th on the bill or summat, we sold so many of our "for all the fucked-up children of this world" t-shirts that we were the seventh-best selling merchandise of the festival. I remember it was a windy day and the sound on stage was blown around a lot, making it quite

**Burning the beer cups**

strange. I hate playing in daylight too, but it seems that over the years dozens of folk have told me that it was their first intro to Spacemen 3 and they dug it, so even without our lightshow it seems we managed to convert a few. I remember watching New Order with Peter Hook and his ridiculously lo-slung bass – he doesn't appear to be able to reach that far now.... Their set was great – very much their ecstasy height.'
**Sonic Boom (Spacemen 3 – guitar/organ/vocals)**

'It was a beautiful weekend – the sun shone brightly. Apart from the one hour when we were scheduled to play. Just for that one hour only, a bloody great rain cloud parked itself over the stage – nowhere else – and pissed on the assembled throng without mercy from first chord to last. Nobody left, nobody ran for shelter. It was a bit like the scene in *Paint Your Wagon* with the Nitty Gritty Dirt Band "Hand Me Down That Can Of Beans"! Mud, rain, everyone jumping around like Stig of the Dump.... I looked out at one point and saw this brown writhing mass with steam rising everywhere like smoke from a fire!'
**Paul Simmonds (The Men They Couldn't Hang – Guitar/ Bouzouki Mandolin/Keyboards)**

'I play when/where I'm asked, I don't really chase, and I was only asked to do Reading twice. One of the years was when the Pogues were on the main stage and I remember being backstage, marvelling at Mr McGowan's capacity to drink the undrinkable (I only drink real ale, which meant that everything he was drinking was undrinkable to me, and there was certainly a lot of it!)'
**Attila the Stockbroker (Vocals/Violin/Crumhorn/Recorder)**

# 1990

**As an indie-festival, the weekend grew and attracted many more 'cool' bands. From the Cramps only appearance, to the first headline slot for the Pixies, the festival couldn't lose, and with the Inspiral Carpets headlining Saturday (with or without Noel Gallagher as one half of a pantomime cow) the resurgence in popularity of the Reading Festival was confirmed.**

'I remember the crowd chanting "you fat bastard" at me. I think it was some current television or football reference, apparently meant as a compliment to me, but I don't know. That's just what someone told me.'
**Black Francis (Pixies – Vocals/Guitar)**

"The show started with a dancing pantomime cow and fireworks (at the beginning of the show, yes!) and a spirited performance. Now with the airbrushing of history and fashions, only fans remember the triumph it was. On a personal note, I got a limousine to ferry my parents from Oxford to the festival and home. The nice people from the Mean Fiddler looked after them, and John Peel bought my father a Guinness, the two most influential males in my life meeting right there at that exact moment of my life. In the early eighties, when Reading was a rock festival, I used to sell bootleg t-shirts outside. It's funny having been on both sides of the fence, working in the music industry at the bottom and the top in the same place.'
**Tom Hingley (Inspiral Carpets – Vocals)**

'My biggest and best memory was closing the main stage on the Saturday night. We'd been surprised at the vast fee we were to receive, so spent loads on the stage show. We let off a few grands' worth of fireworks during the first song (nice touch that, it's usually the end of the gig when the rockets go off). I don't know if it's legend but story has it that the pantomime cow that was dancing on stage with us had our roadie Noel (Gallagher) in its back end.

'As we ended the gig, our special effects people made it snow. Apparently, this completely blew the minds of several thousand attendees who were "under the influence". All in all, a definite pinnacle of our career.'
**Clint Boon (Inspiral Carpets – Keyboards/Vocals)**

'What I remember most was the backstage area... which is where I stayed for most of the time. But that was okay, because the area was huge. It was extremely social, there was plenty to eat and drink, and was really a party in itself.

What contributed to this was the fact that backstage security was extremely lax, meaning it wasn't just a "band and press" area. I found myself hanging out with more than a few wild types who had just come to see the festival.'
**Billy Gould (Faith No More – Bass)**

'I remember mud, lots of mud, mud being thrown. I felt if anyone deserved to be pelted with mud it would be Faith No More. None came.
Nick Cave's book *And the Ass Saw the Angel* had just come out and I was in awe. He played "Black Betty" in a tent and it was really hot and a totally inappropriate hour to be seeing his act.'
**Roddy Bottum (Faith No More – Keyboards)**

'It was a gorgeous, sunny day – which is quite rare for Reading Festival. As usual, John Peel introduced all the bands on the main stage and there's no denying that our hearts started pounding when we heard him use the phrase "Here's The Wedding Present". Our set was mainly composed of songs from our album, *Bizarro*, which had been released the previous year. We received a silver disc for that album and now we were one position away from headlining the Reading Festival. It'd be safe to say that we felt like we'd arrived.

'After The Wedding Present, Inspiral Carpets played, and their performance was dazzling... a breathtaking light show, a huge fireworks display, drum majorettes... I think they must've spent most of their fee on the stage show. But the next day they were completely blown away by The Pixies performing in the same slot. They were just four odd-looking people standing on stage playing rock music without any theatrics or gimmicks. But they didn't need any. The sheer power and quality of the music was more than enough.'
**David Gedge (The Wedding Present – Vocals/Guitar)**

'I recall our set being enjoyable enough (to us at least!). We even had to convey a safety message, which had always been a slight ambition of mine. But the incident that really caught the day was having my golf swing assessed by the Mayor of Pangbourne. He'd especially gone to the festival to see

THE MEAN FIDDLER PRESENTS

## THE 1990 READING FESTIVAL

AUGUST BANK HOLIDAY WEEKEND

FRI 24th AUGUST     SAT 25th AUGUST     SUN 26th AUGUST

### THE CRAMPS
FAITH NO MORE

NICK CAVE
& THE
BAD SEEDS
MUDHONEY
JANES ADDICTION
MEGACITY 4
AN EMOTIONAL FISH
FROM 2PM

### INSPIRAL CARPETS
THE WEDDING PRESENT

THE BUZZCOCKS
BILLY BRAGG
RIDE
THE YOUNG GODS
THE CHILLS
PERE UBU
PSYCHIC TV
FROM 12 NOON

### PIXIES
THE FALL
JESUS JONES
TACK-HEAD
LOOP
LIVING COLOUR
STEREO MC'S
THE TELESCOPES
THEE HYPNOTICS
THE SENSELESS THINGS
FROM 12 NOON

COMPERE JOHN PEEL

◆MEAN FIDDLER STAGE◆

Nick Cave and the
Bad Seeds bring
some Aussie warmth
to the main stage

Tom Robinson (I think it was) and he'd obviously blagged his way into the backstage area (probably the robe and chains I suspect) and was ligging with anyone he could. Sad to report the episode's conclusion involved the ubiquitous "Incident Tape" and a story in the following week's Thames Valley Chronicle. It was stated that my name was Kurtis Cobham (though to be fair I did tell him that) and that I'd called him a "Chubby Roustabout". Verily, them were the days....'
**Nigel Blackwell (Half Man, Half Biscuit – Vocals/Guitar)**

'It is possible that Reading was the best gig I ever had in my life, but I simply remember absolutely nothing about it.'
**Luka Bloom (Vocals/Guitar)**

'My boyfriend at the time suggested it would be a good idea, so we found an advert in *NME* for the Mean Fiddler Events Company and booked our tickets on the telephone. I seem to remember it cost about £45.00 each for the weekend. I received my "A" Level results on the Thursday and found I had passed and had a place at my chosen uni. We set off on the train from Plymouth and arrived on the Friday, the station was awash with festival goers and our next stop was the local Co-Op. We stocked up on beer and toilet rolls, loads of the shelves were empty of booze and tinned supplies! We arrived and pitched our tent and quickly organised our first "smoke". In fact, I think it was crumbled in coffee! The Pixies were on that year and the Inspiral Carpets and James. The atmosphere was amazing – from hippies to students to travellers. I remember the Saturday night. My boyfriend collapsed onto the floor, hitting his legs shouting "They are on fire, they're on fire!" which of course they weren't. How we ever found our way back to our tent amazed me, among the sea of tents. I remember the sad feeling when we left on the Sunday, mixed with the longing to get home and get bathed! It felt like I had just experienced something quite amazing.'
**Kirstin Tellum (Festival Virgin)**

**Miles Hunt takes a well needed rest**

Black Francis of the Pixies

After the ball is over!

Take the long way home

# 1991

**With no apparent competition from other festivals, Reading began to thrive and introduce more diverse acts such as De La Soul and the first festival appearance by Blur. The inclusion of PWEI, Carter USM and Ned's Atomic Dustbin on the main stage saw a 'grebo' revolution, which almost obscured the festival debut of a small band from Seattle, on the damp Friday afternoon. Who were they? A band called Nirvana: grunge had arrived in Berkshire.**

'It was the moment that our credibility and popularity converged and peaked. For at least one hour in a field in Berkshire, Carter The Unstoppable Sex Machine were the most popular and fantastic rock group in the whole wide world. It was like the Nuremberg Rally for nice people.

'My memories from the day are of Jon Fat Beast introducing us in his Minnie Mouse costume, of erecting our great new expensive lightshow upside down, and in particular all the rumours that we spread. In the days before the Leeds Festival we could spend three days at Reading, watching our favourite bands, trying to blag free drink from the American press tent and, best of all, we had the whole weekend to start a good festival lie.

'A tall tale told backstage on a Friday would have two days to spread its way round 40,000 people and find its way back to us before we left on the Sunday. My favourite rumour was that Cliff Richard had died – not particularly funny – but great to hear someone else ask you "Have you heard about Cliff?" when it was you that had made it up in the first place the day before.'
**Jim Bob (Carter the Unstoppable Sex machine – Vocals/Guitar)**

'I remember riding into town in our Renault Espace and being amazed by just how many Carter shirts there were on the backs of punters heading for the festival site. I also remember winding down the window and telling all the crusties to "go get a job".

'The lead-up to our time on stage was pretty effortless for me and Jim Bob, but behind the scenes the "Crazy Carter Crew" were working like mad. The backstage area was a frenzy of amps, guitars, leads, lights and four-letter words. After all those efforts, the stage was set, the sound was right, the lights went on and there, above the stage in huge letters, were the words CARTER USM... upside down.

'We stepped on stage just as the sun was setting, the sky was amazing. More amazing, though, was the huge crowd. It was my first experience of a big festval crowd and it felt like I was being born again. All through my teens I had had a picture in my mind's eye of what it would be like when I became "famous" – and here it was, that very moment. I remember, during a quiet passage of a song, looking out at the festival, watching a train glide past, the moon rising up from the horizon, and seeing a swaying glow of lighters held up by the crowd who were singing along en masse to one of our songs. In that split second, in a field in Reading, all was right with the world.'
**Les 'Fruitbat' Carter (Carter the Unstoppable Sex Machine – Guitar)**

'Witnessing the first appearance of Nirvana just a few minutes before being collared by John Peel for an onsite radio interview, I was able to tell him about this amazing unknown American band I'd just seen blow the roof off. The Reading Festival was always the best place to spend quality time with him. Usually sat cross-legged on the grass in the backstage enclosure with his wife, Sheila, and various offspring by his side. A lovely man. Sadly missed but with us forever.

'Seeing Iggy after a typically nihilistic headline set, hardly able to walk, talk, breathe, being carried down the ramp offstage by bodyguards, but still insisting on spending two minutes with a young boy (only nine or ten years old) who'd been waiting eagerly at the bottom of the ramp for his autograph.'
**Clint Boon (Inspiral Carpets – Keyboards/Vocals)**

'I can't remember all that much about the gig itself, I think we went down well, but I'd had two e's and a bag of mushrooms before we went on and they all sort of kicked in on the second song, after that I was flying! That was probably chickenfeed compared to the amount the rest of Flowered Up had consumed by then.

'Other memories include Damon Albarn wishing me a good gig before we went on and my girlfriend at the time chewing the ear off Bobby Gillespie. Apart from that, I'm pretty sure a good time was had by all.'
**Tim Dorney (Flowered Up – Keyboards)**

92

RIGHT: Fruit Bat of Carter USM
during a triumphant special guest set

BELOW: Jim Bob from Carter USM
points to the heights he wants his
band to reach

'I had been a Nirvana fan since the beginning, because they were out of Seattle and I still maintained strong ties there, particularly via my friend Charles Peterson, who regularly sent me care packages with all the Sub Pop singles. I loved Bleach, but had never seen them live and was really excited. What I saw that day was an epiphany. It was clear as day that no one was going to surpass their performance, and that they were headed for world domination. It wasn't just me – a lot of folks I talked to at the time felt the same way.'
**Steve Mack (That Petrol Emotion – Vocals)**

'I never went to any of the Reading Festivals. Residents dreaded the arrival of "the great unwashed" and I used to avoid the area, primarily because of traffic congestion!"
**Marion Chappell (Tilehurst Webmistress)**

'As far as the festival, it was a lot of negotiating getting there. It was a big hassle whenever we played... so I didn't get to see a lot of bands. Being younger, it just seemed harder to negotiate, to navigate things mentally; you were just more involved in playing.'
**Murph (Dinosaur Jr – Drums)**

**BELOW: Welcome the festival
– leave your 'bad attitude' at the entrance**

**RIGHT: I'm lost and alone, in a field full of crap!**

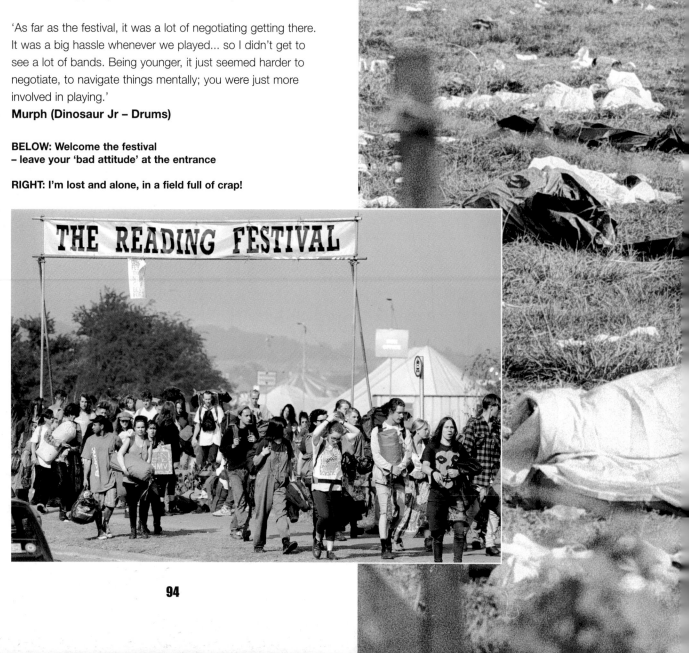

# 1992

A year on from their debut and Nirvana were headlining. With their *Nevermind* album hitting triple platinum sales in the US alone, they were the biggest band on the planet, but would they turn up to play? Cobain arrived, pushed onstage in a wheelchair, in a hospital gown and blond wig, and the band proceeded to play one of the most memorable headlining slots at the festival ever. Grunge was also apparent right across the bill with Melvins, Mudhoney and Screaming Trees appearing over the weekend, with all the acts on the Sunday main stage bill chosen by Cobain himself.

'Mark Radcliffe and I had been working together for just about a year when he was invited to present the bands in the *NME* tent at the Reading Festival. He asked me if I fancied tagging along so we could eat, drink and be merry together. Nirvana were to headline the main stage and due to Kurt's precarious mental state the big question hanging over the weekend was "will Cobain turn up"? Krist Novoselic was knocking around backstage, so the signs were good. Then the rumour circulated that Cobain was in hospital.

'Come Sunday night the site was a quagmire and the Nirvana gossip had hit its peak. I remember Mark introduced the last band in the tent and we headed over to the main attraction. We flashed our AAA passes and took to the stage, alongside John Peel. The atmosphere was unbelievable and I'll never forget the rhythm section taking the stage and then the famous arrival of Cobain – in a long blonde wig and hospital gown being steered right past us in his wheelchair by Everett True. He hurled himself out of the chair and kick-started what is probably the best gig I've ever seen. At the end of the show he smashed his guitar... which landed at my feet. It was a copy of the guitar he'd been playing throughout the gig – which surprised me a little. I toyed with the idea of picking the battered plank up – but considering myself far too cool to get involved in such fandom, I left it. Someone else picked it up. It went at auction about five years later, $6,000.'

**Marc Riley (Lard-BBC 6 Music DJ)**

'It's quite bizarre, really. Nirvana were in Australia, in Melbourne, in early 1992 when they had just had a hit with "Teen Spirit" and they were touring on the back of that. I don't quite know how they heard about our gig in a suburb next to where they were doing their show, but they showed up and bought all of our t-shirts that we had on sale, which was remarkable. Then we saw Dave Grohl was wearing a Bjorn Again t-shirt on an interview on TV!!! It was completely mad.

'Then I think it was mainly down to Kurt Cobain, which is what I understand from all the reports. He said specifically to the Reading Festival organisers he didn't want any "limey" bands playing, he wanted so many American bands and Bjorn Again. 'We set up on the day and we were invited in to meet the guys from Nirvana – Krist, Dave and Kurt – and we said thanks very much and it was so great to be here and it was fantastic for us. I said to the guys that when the girls go off and do a costume change, we explore the darker side of ABBA. I said to Kurt Cobain "look, you're headlining tonight so we'll drop "Smells Like Teen Spirit"" and he said "no, you've got to do it, it'll be fantastic." I thought shit; this is going to be awful, us doing their song and the crowd going "Booooo. Fuck off!!!!!" We thought okay, we've got to try it.

'So we came on and did our normal set. "Waterloo". The crowd were eyeing us up and down and saying "what the heck is this?" but we had them by the third song. When we did "Smells Like Teen Spirit" everyone went crazy, wearing the costumes made it all accessible.
We watched L7, who we had met up with before in America, and the Beastie Boys as well, it was just a great day.'

**Rutger Sonofagunn (Bjorn Again – Bass)**

**Abba 're-Bjorn'**

**97**

Kurt Cobain provides one of the
festival's classic performances

Manic Street Preachers playing at
Reading for the last time as a four piece

'When Therapy? got offered first on the main stage we leapt at the chance and arranged to stay on for the Sunday, so as we could catch a lot of our favourite bands playing that day. On arrival, we were shown our portakabin/dressing room and given our passes. Our dressing room was beside Henry Rollins, a hero of ours, who sat outside reading a book. This impressed us no end. I have very lucid memories of the gig and enjoyed every minute I was on stage. We got to see Melvins, Pavement, Teenage Fanclub, Mudhoney and, of course, Nirvana. We watched Nirvana from way back in the field and I remember the sound was blowing all over the place, but the volume of the crowd singing along to the songs was immense.'
**Andy Cairns (Therapy? – Vocals/Guitar)**

'I did attend as a backstage guest and got to see fledgling Suede perform in a tent, along with Ian McCulloch and Will Sergeant's vastly under-rated new band, Electrafixion. I also saw Tricky on the main stage and with the state I was in at the time that was the highlight of the weekend for me. And I did get to see Nirvana also.'
**Wayne Hussey (The Mission – Vocals/Guitar)**

'If the truth be known, we weren't big fans of festivals. There was definitely a Mod ethic in the band, which associated festivals with hippies, middle-class rebellion, and mud! Remember, this was 1992, festival fever hadn't yet gripped the nation and big business hadn't realised the enormous marketing potential of a field full of graduates. We were Situationists, some of us followers of Guy Debord, we were attracted to the concept of anarchy, so we hatched a plan. The first idea was to arrive at the festival on scooters, in full Mod regalia. Then we heard that Public Enemy were playing, so we thought, lets get the local chapter of Hells Angels to escort us as Mods into the festival and watch those cats stare!

'Then, Plan B was hatched. We would arrive in limos with a traffic-stopping police escort, all dressed in black, with replica guns stuffed in our pockets. This is how we arrived. Sunglasses with attitude! It was ALL MEANT TO BE A MASSIVE PISS TAKE.

'Nobody got the joke. Mick Jones (who was playing with Big Audio Dynamite at the festival) saw us whisked into the backstage area, commenting "Flash Bastards". Even our mates didn't get it. We had a brilliant time backstage. Journalists ducked and ran for their lives, as Keith Mullin discharged his blank firing Magnum. It was another "irony" sketch which fed our perverse sense of humour. It was a

hilarious attempt at exposing the hypocrisy of journalists toadying to the likes of Public Enemy, who also ran for cover. Keith Mullin became the hardest man in rock... it was anarchy, it was the reason we had joined a band. I look back at Reading 1992 with fond memories, but also remember it was the time we finally realised we needed therapy!'
**Peter Hooton (The Farm – Vocals)**

'It was the year that Seattle came to Reading. Nirvana, the Screaming Trees, Mudhoney, the whole crew were there. Not only that, but tons of friends from Seattle came over to join the party. It was like a punk rock high school reunion. Great performances all around, and much merriment, but what I really remember was the hotel where virtually everyone was staying. Word had gotten out and the hotel bar had turned into a huge party. The hotel employees were starting to get nervous, as there were obviously far more people in the hotel than was safe at this point, and no one had any plans to leave any time soon. To their credit, they decided just to keep the bar open, and to let things run their course. And boy, did they run their course.

'This led to one of my dearest memories of England, and shows just how different our cultures are. At the end of the night, when people had passed out from exhaustion, drinking – or both – the halls were littered with bodies, as people who didn't have hotel rooms colonized any available bit of floor space. I can clearly remember hotel employees wandering the halls with extra blankets, tucking people in. That's something you would never see here in the good ol' USA – we all would have been thrown in jail.'
**Steve Mack (That Petrol Emotion – Vocals)**

'My own favourite festival memory is waiting for four hours at the front to see Nirvana headline. It was all a bit of a haze, but watching Kurt wheeled on stage in a white smock, I remember this rush of recognition that this was a historical moment. Asking us to say "we love you Courtney" for him to record also made me feel that here was a man who wasn't just a living icon, but actually a human being!'
**Linda Serck (BBC Radio Berkshire – DJ)**

'I remember getting ready in a tent and feeling like a clown in a circus: putting on my clown makeup, wig and costume. Only thing missing was the red nose. We had a good crowd when we played. I think one of the most insane magical intense things besides getting to play the famous festival ourselves was Nirvana playing.

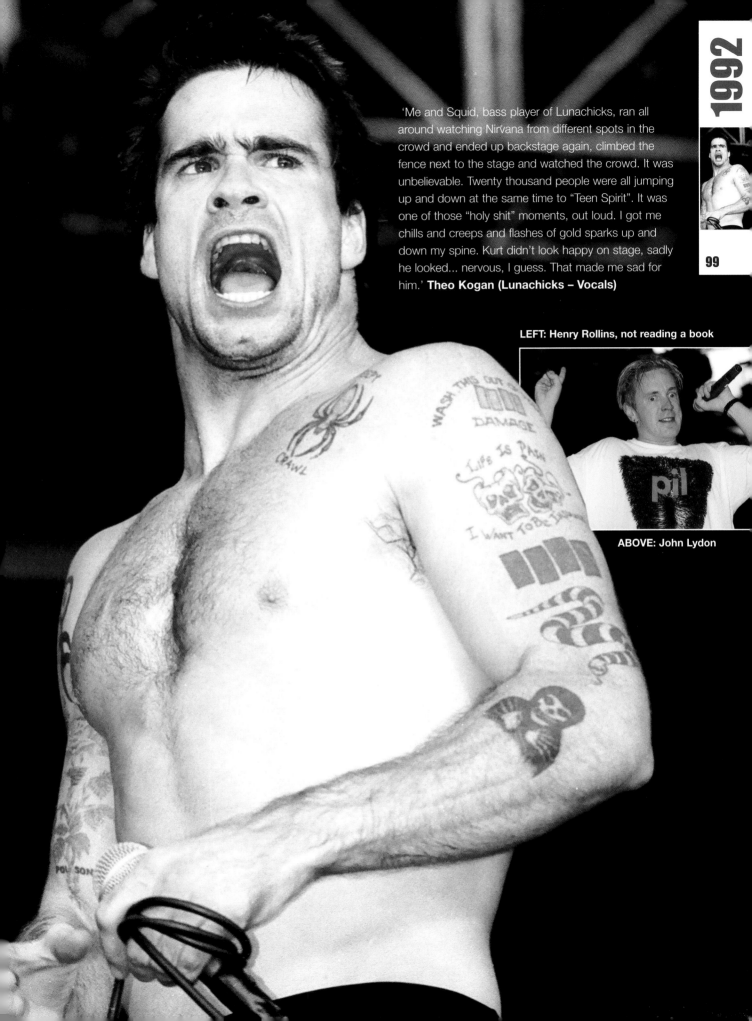

'Me and Squid, bass player of Lunachicks, ran all around watching Nirvana from different spots in the crowd and ended up backstage again, climbed the fence next to the stage and watched the crowd. It was unbelievable. Twenty thousand people were all jumping up and down at the same time to "Teen Spirit". It was one of those "holy shit" moments, out loud. I got me chills and creeps and flashes of gold sparks up and down my spine. Kurt didn't look happy on stage, sadly he looked... nervous, I guess. That made me sad for him.' **Theo Kogan (Lunachicks – Vocals)**

LEFT: Henry Rollins, not reading a book

ABOVE: John Lydon

# 1993

Not such a good year for headline bands, but a fantastic supporting cast. Rage Against the Machine went crazy with their 'Agit-pop rock' and Fishbone laid down some funky grooves on the Sunday afternoon, basking in the 'Everyday Sunshine'. Elsewhere, Blur proved to be the forerunners of the new Brit Pop movement and Radiohead made their festival debut in the *NME/Melody Maker* tent.

'A large chunk of the crowd knew our songs and were singing them back at us, which was very thrilling indeed. Our bass player, Michael, had in the previous week's *Kerrang!* mag done a band-by-band appraisal of the other acts on at the weekend, so we were greeted with a certain animosity in some quarters. Michael's article was very tongue-in-cheek and certainly not meant to offend, however, bands like Butthole Surfers took it all very badly indeed and Gibby Haines, the frontman, was very vocal on and off the stage about "kicking our ass" etc. The Chinese whispers meant that nearly every other band thought we had a beef with them, even though they hadn't even read the article in question.'
**Andy Cairns (Therapy? – Vocals/Guitar)**

'I do remember that the weather was fantastic, and we were greeted at the artist entrance by some dude covered in tattoos, wearing a kilt, which he immediately lifted to show us his full Prince Albert. We were on first on the "big" stage, and I kinda remember feeling a bit strange; like we were waking everyone up. It seemed to go over pretty well, although I'm

pretty sure no one except the half-dozen Japanese girls in the front had any clue who we were. And maybe even they thought we were someone else.

'But by far the best part of the whole weekend was seeing Big Star. Gigolo Aunts absolutely worshipped that band, and to see them play was fantastic. We knew the guys in the Posies, so were able to say hello and meet Alex Chilton. Who promptly offered me a joint. Which I smoked. Without sharing. Like an idiot. But he didn't seem to mind at all, and just rolled another one, all the while asking us about our various star signs.'
**Dave Gibbs (Gigolo Aunts – Vocals/Guitar)**

'Reading – legendary in the sense that its history outweighed the befuddled, muddied commonplace of its reality. A festival everyone wanted to play, because of its legacy. Slade were re-born there. Umpteen bands got mud chucked at 'em there. Bikers went there. That's it. That's the history I knew about the festival. I loved it. I love playing legendary places, places with heavy significance. I love rock 'n' roll.... But it has to prove itself first.

**Hello! From the front of the stage**

**Spotlight on Siouxsie**

'The year we played there, we were on the "up" as it were. We'd never had a tour bus, but we looked in envy at the bands we knew who'd graduated to the hallowed double-decker sleeper bus. They rolled into the site at night, parked where they wanted, and sank into the mud. And slept there, in their comfortable bunks. We trundled in late afternoon, a minibus full of northern oiks drinking spirits and wondering what was going on. We were here to say something, to use the platform. This was 1993, and the UK was awash with Tory policies and far-right thugs. We wandered around google-eyed at the backstage freebies. Whoo. We'd never seen this stuff before. Free sandwiches... We played on the second stage, sometime after Credit to the Nation and just before some big indie band of the time. We felt separate, different. We always did. We loved rock 'n' roll, loved music, loved crowds... but somewhere along the line we missed the bit where you have to be a coke-fuelled ego-maniac to really "rock that crowd".

'So we played, and it was great. Back to the Planet were playing that night, I remember. The audience, the people who'd come to see us at the festival, they were great. Brilliant. I swapped stories with the lovely guitarist from Back to the Planet, who'd put his dirty sneakers into the microwave to dry them and had his kitchen explode.'
**Boff Whalley (Chumbawamba – Vocals/Guitar)**

'Our first UK appearance. LOTS of burning plastic bonfires… during the Big Star set, despite the fact that New Order were playing their farewell show on the main stage at the same time, I remember the side of the stage as Big Star performed

was coated with musos… J Mascis, Evan Dando, Juliana Hatfield and many others…. We hadn't played much as Big Star, in fact I think Reading was our third show. I barely remember the Posies set, as it was our first show in the UK. I believe we were fairly wide-eyed, probably a bit nervous.'
**Ken Stringfellow (The Posies – Vocals/Guitar/Keyboards)**

'I don't remember but I'm quite sure I was there. Where is the Reading Festival? Is it in the UK?'
**Angelo Moore (Fishbone – Vocals/Saxophone/Theramin/Percussion)**

'I'm pretty sure I might have taken mushrooms that day. I had a good time, of course. It's just kind of a blurry memory.'
**John Norwood Fisher (Fishbone – Bass/Vocals)**

'You probably weren't aware of it – most people weren't – but for the three days of August Bank Holiday in 1993 I was the King of Reading. I had crowned myself in a fit of backstage-paddock euphoria on the first balmy night of the festival and my stupid but benign regal fantasy sort of caught on amongst the hedonistic clique I was running with in those days.

'To set the scene: I was a music journalist then, hitting a peak as far as committed festival attendance was concerned. I loved the festivals in those days. I was single, self-sufficient, under 30 and lengthy of hair, and the early nineties were a great time to be all of those things. I wore boots and band-logo t-shirts and those long indie shorts. I carried my personal effects in an army surplus handbag. In the summer months I wore a voluminous, long-sleeved Cure top tied around my waist, which made an instant picnic blanket for sitting on grass. Contrary to my rather unkempt, studenty look I was in gainful employment: Features Editor of the culturally voracious *Select* magazine.

'Perhaps we were just desperate for kicks during a fallow period for music. Having seen Public Enemy, the Manics and Nirvana at Reading '92, the prospect of Porno For Pyros headlining Friday night didn't exactly sound legendary on paper (not having already closed Glastonbury two months earlier), nor, to be brutal, did old-timers like Siouxsie & The Banshees, The The and New Order. But in the event it was my favourite ever Reading. Everything just came together. The feeling that the abundance of witty Ned's, Kingmaker and Senseless Things t-shirts around the site "meant" something. The fact that throughout the weekend the focal point was intermittently the *Melody Maker* tent – The Frank & Walters,

Blur, Radiohead, Back To The Planet, Boo Radleys – not the main stage. The amazing line-up on the Subterrania Dance Stage at the Rivermead Centre (M People, Inner City, The Grid), because indie kids had learned to dance during Acid House and they weren't about to stop. The way the sun shone during Therapy?'s grimly fiendish heavy metal set on the Saturday afternoon but it didn't take the edge off it. The way old-timers New Order sounded on the Sunday night – that is, magisterial – blowing Americans like Dinosaur Jr and Fishbone out of the water in a symbolic display of British sea power.

'Over that Bank Holiday I came to realise why, sometimes, Reading is better than Glastonbury. Sure, it lacks ley-lines and healing fields and men on stilts, but that merely concentrates the mind. It's all about the music. It has to be. It doesn't have anything else to offer. Other than ease of access, of course. You can turn up by train and walk to the site. Equally, as I did when the storm clouds formed overhead the year previously, you can walk off the site without a moment's forward planning and get the hell out of there. In doing so, I missed Kurt Cobain being pushed onstage in a wheelchair and what was a legendary Nirvana set. But you can't have everything. Even if you are the king. (Andrew Collins is no longer King of Reading.)'
**Andrew Collins (DJ/Author)**

'Upon arrival in the morning we seemed to be the only band that didn't have a proper tour bus, even though the vehicle we had was larger than any other we'd toured in. Moments later, we were drinking Jack Daniels with the Jesus Lizard (and I don't even like Jack and especially not in the morning). I was really impressed with how smoothly the crew ran the show. Of course, they've been doing it for years.... Everything was on wheels and they just rotated the band gear like it was on a huge turntable. We were completely miked and line-checked a good two hours before we hit. It was sweet.

'It was by far the biggest gig we'd ever played and though it seemed like a fluke that we were on the main stage, the crowd went nuts. The roar of the crowd when I played "War Pigs" on the trombone was deafening. New Order was the headliner that evening (the only British band on the bill) and I remember having to be asked several times to "please don't lean on my car". They drove up in individual BMWs to the backstage area. Very special indeed.'
**Stephen Moses (Alice Donut – Drums/Trombone)**

'Even Alex Chilton seemed to have fun.'
**Peter Visser (Betty Serveert – Guitar)**

'We played the tent and it was more "rammed" than was safe and one guy decided to climb up the guide poles.... He climbed up about 15 feet and was then throwing himself off and landing on people's necks and then doing it again. We were just watching people, pale teenagers, being dragged from the crowd, which was really off-putting as you're trying to play! Then the guy climbing up the pole pulled out a rope and there was a fear that the marquee was going to collapse. Security came to the side of the stage and spoke to our manager, saying "you've got to pull the gig", but he said "if you don't let them do Eject, there's going to be a riot." But we managed to play it and then had to leave pretty soon after as they cleared the marquee. For hours after we kept seeing people in neck-braces around the site."
**Nick Michaelson (Senser – Guitar)**

'There was one man who had neck-brace on who'd been off and came back for the end of the gig! Basically, he'd been crushed by the guy landing on his neck.'
**Kerstin Haigh (Senser – Vocals/Flute)**

'Our earlier band Sub Sub played in the Leisure Centre next to the site. It was billed as the Reading aftershow gig. It was shite. The best thing about that was going to the hotel where the headliners' stay and partying with New Order.'
**Jimi Goodwin (Doves – Vocals/Bass/Guitar/Drums)**

**A dry afternoon at the festival**

EAN FIDD

PRESENTS

ADINC

Looking up at the Main Stage

MEAN FIDDLER

PRESENTS

READING 93

MEAN FIDDLER

PRESENTS

READING 93

# 1994

**Talking point of the whole weekend was Courtney Love's implosion on the main stage, where she appeared to be in the throws of a nervous breakdown, in the aftermath of Kurt Cobain's death the previous April. Otherwise, a fantastic line-up, with the first headline appearance of the Red Hot Chili Peppers and more Brit Pop than you could shake a stick at with Sleeper, Salad, Echobelly, Elastica, Lush, Gene and more. The Manic Street Preachers played the main stage on the Sunday as a three piece, for the first time, due to Richey Edwards' absence.**

'There's no denying that it was easier to play on the smaller stage than it was on the main stage. As headliners, the crowd was mainly composed of our fans and the atmosphere was electric. But there is always part of you that hankers to take on 40,000 people!

'Earlier in the day I bumped into an old journalist friend, Everett True, who was backstage with Courtney Love. He beckoned me over because he wanted to introduce me to Courtney, and as an enormous fan of her band, Hole, I wasn't about to refuse. But as I approached them I could tell that Courtney seemed, as they say, a little tired and emotional. After Everett had presented me she slurred "Aren't you friends with Steve Albini?" After I'd said 'Yes… well... kind of, anyway…" she responded by slapping me playfully across the face and telling me that I was "very naughty". The following day, apart from being interviewed by a young up-and-coming Signal Radio DJ called Chris Moyles, I had to make my way to the "Bud Dry" tent, where presenters from over 30 American radio stations had established little studios and interviewing desks. The first question I was ever asked in an American interview was: "David… do you expect the unexpected?"'
**David Gedge (The Wedding Present – Vocals/Guitar)**

'I played in the afternoon, during one of my solo career lows, and received a rather indifferent reaction from the audience. Just because a big rock festival goes on and on just like Christmas, it doesn't mean that the artist has lovely memories of the experience.'
**Frank Black (Frank Black – Vocals/Guitar)**

'We were billed as third from top, but Soundgarden pulling out put us on just before the Chilli Peppers, when it was getting dark. The crowd were amazing, we played out of our skin and we got really to enjoy the festival. It also opened our eyes to the power of a great festival set. Before we went on stage our latest album *Troublegum* had reached silver status in the UK. Shortly after our Reading performance, it went gold.'
**Andy Cairns (Therapy? – Vocals/Guitar)**

'The weather was superb those first couple days. We'd hop the train out to Reading and follow the ant trail of young hipsters out to the grounds with our "artist" laminates clamped between sweaty fingers. We loitered around the special backstage area, drinking Carlsberg lager in the sun, reconnecting with old friends, meeting new ones, and spotting famous people. There were too many high points to mention. Among the highest was being introduced by Scott Booker to the near-numinous John Peel while whooping it up with the Flaming Lips. We also spent much of our time with WHFS' Johnny Riggs, and our Superchunk friends.

'I do remember it was finally raining. Mark and I wandered around the various booths and spectacles; there seemed to be some attempt made at a group hug or it might have been some type of fight. We bought military surplus jackets to fend off the rain and wandered back to our backstage "singlewide" where the Erics and our venerable tour manager and friend Enda were waiting. The mood became serious. We hammered out a set list, tuned instruments, and gathered behind the *Melody Maker* stage to wait our turn. Eric J suggested we thank the *NME* for letting us play. We all felt that would be funny, because that's the kind of thing we found funny.

'Eric Johnson somehow convinced me I should announce it, probably because I'm the band idiot, and I think those were the first words out of my mouth: "We'd like to thank the *NME* for having us play." One of the bouncers turned around and, in a voice like the flexing doo-rag wearing guys from Monty Python declared "It's Me-Lo-Dee Ma-Kaah!" The ice was broken. For the first time, I noticed the crowd. Fucking immense. That was the largest crowd I have ever played in front of. I was so nervous, I was dizzy. The rain and beer-soaked throng steamed like a cauldron.'
**Matt Gentling (Archers of Loaf – Bass)**

'Playing Reading that year was really the event that made me realise we were onto something big. We consciously wore our "RRRRock" clothes, a little middle finger to the shoe-gazing

*NME* indie twats who were associated with Reading around that time. Our Reading t-shirt "Fuck you and Fuck your tent" was a bestseller and led to the arrest of one wearer in Reading town centre.... And, as ever for Terrorvision, the sun shone for the gig and started to dip behind the horizon as we left the stage.'
**Leigh Marklew (Terrorvision – Bass)**

'My Dad took me. I was about 13 years old and Red Hot Chili Peppers were headlining. Soundgarden pulled out, which was a big let down for me. I also recall seeing They Might Be Giants, not through personal choice, but he dragged me there. It was the first time that I saw my Dad using expletives on a regular basis, using his elbows to stop anyone getting past him to see the bands, he was an experienced "gig goer". I remember being blown away by, in particular, the Chili Peppers. They gave me the hunger to go back the next year and opened my eyes up to music.'
**Ben Gautrey (The Cooper Temple Clause
– Guitar/Bass/Keyboards /Vocals)**

'Courtney Love played with Hole right after Kurt Cobain's death. No one could even believe she was going to be able to perform but she was there. I even think it might have been her first public appearance since his death. I just remember the feeling of voyeurism that was so present. Everyone

**Red Hot Chili Peppers headline the festival**

wanted to see the train wreck. Would she be pissed or psycho? Would she break down in tears or scream her way through the set? It almost seemed like people were hoping for a little drama that they could take home to their friends.

'People were talking about her and sniffing around for news about her, but I don't think anyone just went up to her and said "Hi". I am just as guilty. I wanted to see her play and I think part of it was morbid fascination, but I wish I had maybe just smiled at her and waved or something."
**Tracey Belland (Voice of the Beehive – Vocals/Guitar)**

'First time we played we were way down the list on the second stage, but ripped it up and included a blistering version of The Beatles' "Don't Let Me Down". We were signed soon after and were hot shit for a year or so.'
**Kevin Miles (Gene – Bass)**

*Courtney Love*

'I recall it was a beautiful clear breezy Sunday. The band hit around 4pm to another busting-at-the-seams tent... the energy between band and audience equalled the beauty of the day... everyone was pulling and feeding off eachother. There was no separation between band and audience.

'After the gig, and for me the highlight of that sunny day, was dancing hand-in-hand for hours off stage with Elizabeth Fraser and her daughter, who was wearing the most beautiful summer dress... an angel from heaven. Hearing them sing English lullabies and joining them in silly games provided a well-needed escape from the touring treadmill....'
**Gene Bowen (Jeff Buckley's Tour Manager)**

'Our bass player jumped into the air on the first note of the first beat of the first song of the set. He must have performed this jump a thousand times before, but on this very public occasion the jump went horribly wrong. Actually, that isn't strictly true. The jump went fine, it was the landing that caused the problem. His kneecap popped completely out of its socket, resulting in one valiant bass player refusing to leave the stage, opting instead to play in more pain than is imaginable.

'I don't know who looked the most green-faced and nauseous, our bassist or the doctor on the side of the stage, yelling at him to come off and receive some immediate medical treatment. Our guy completed the set sitting on a flight case, and afterwards the doctor literally pushed the kneecap back into its rightful place before carting him off to hospital.'
**Ginger (The Wildhearts – Vocals/Guitar)**

'We decided to mark the occasion by playing a medley of "Temple Head" with the ultimate indie-dance crossover track, Primal Scream's "Loaded" which was round about the same tempo. Vocalist Natacha Atlas worked out an Arabic melody line for it while vocalist/MC Neil Sparkes was persuaded to do a Bobby Gillespie impression. This proved a bit difficult, so he decided to do Mick Jagger instead on the grounds that Bobby Gillespie would quite like to have been him.

'This all seemed a very good idea till TGU got on stage and a power surge knocked our equipment out for a minute. When we got it back on, our collection of rather cheap samplers were all playing in different keys. So the audience were treated to a bunch of guys in Nepalese temple masks (which three of

**Blowin' bubbles**

TGU used to wear onstage) running round the stage waving their arms about, a belly dancer singing in Arabic, and a guy in a wig shouting "Where's Keith?" accompanied by some beats and some atonal noise. Some of the crowd thought it was deliberate and loved it – the rest went to the bar.'
**Tim Whelan (Trans-Global Underground
– Keyboards/Programming)**

'What we were interested in doing was scaring the shit out of the crowd – presenting a show which was madder, more hectic and extreme than the rock bands. We, as a predominately Asian band, were a new concept for the crowd and I am sure many thought we were gonna walk on with Ravi Shankar and play some restaurant music. We were under pressure because doing Reading is not a novelty, it is a prestigious gig – the line up that day of the other bands was awesome.

'I remember walking out and looking at the crowd, you could see a bit of fear but also feel a sense of excitement because without doubt Fun Da Mental was different in many aspects. Guys with turbans on, balaclavas over the face – me with my Palestinian scarf wrapped around like the stone throwers on TV – it was a sight that many had never seen. The two rappers Mushtaq and Hotdog running around like psychos – screaming, shouting and putting their confrontational lyrics right down the throats of the punters. We were firing as a band – the crowd did not go mental. I think they were gobsmacked, but did not take their eyes of us. We walked off the stage without a care whether the audience liked it or not. All we knew was that we performed and showed our passion, not just for the politics but also for the music and the art form. For that brief 45 minutes Reading was more than just a rock festival – it was a representing a change from the sons of immigrants who were vexed to the maximum. To Reading Festival, thanks for the opportunity.'
**Aki Nawaz (Fun Da Mental – Percussion/Producer)**

'What is interesting is that they mix up extremely professional streamlined bands with bands that are literally loading their own equipment onto the stage. For a band like Sebadoh, at that time, we were pretty ramshackle and loading our own stuff, we generally had a soundman. But, you don't know what the protocol is; you don't know how these scary dudes who work on the stage want you to talk to them....'
**Lou Barlow (Sebadoh – Vocals/Guitar)**

# 1995

**Another successful weekend. Neil Young, backed by Pearl Jam (minus Eddie Vedder). The first headline appearance by Smashing Pumpkins, and Bjork was back for the first time since '89, when she played with the Sugarcubes. Elsewhere, the event of the weekend was the debut of Foo Fighters – the band formed by Dave Grohl of Nirvana – which saw huge crowds trying to gain access to the *NME/Melody Maker* tent.**

'Carter played again, this time in the *Melody Maker* tent. Fruitbat had injured his back cleaning his bath and had to do the gig sat in a chair.'
**Jim Bob (Carter the Unstoppable Sex Machine – Vocals/Guitar)**

'Headlining the tent in 1995, feeling like Maria Callas with flowers at my feet.'
**Martin Rossiter (Gene – Vocals)**

'We headlined the *Melody Maker* tent, which was great, and got some free Doc Martins!!!'
**Kevin Miles (Gene – Bass)**

'Gene had just played the *NME/Melody Maker* stage and David Grohl's new band the Foo Fighters were playing after us. I wanted to see this performance at close range, so decided to stay on stage. About two minutes before show time the Fighters congregated stage right and I was within hearing distance of the pre-gig pep talk. It consisted simply of David saying "Okay, ready?". Nods of relaxed agreement all round and then BOOM!

'I will never forget the noise of the crowd when the band hit the stage. The title fight was won in that split second. The band was awesome and the tent went absolutely fucking nuts. Mayhem is an understatement. The tent was so oversubscribed that people were hurtling over the front stage barriers, reminiscent of scenes from *Gallipoli*. From my vantage point I could see everything and I was scared for myself and the people at the front. That's how was serious it was. The Reading officials miraculously policed the chaos and the event was injury free.

'I have never witnessed an atmosphere more electric and a band in complete control since and for me that was a defining moment of what the essence of rock'n'roll is.'
**Steve Mason (Gene – Guitar)**

'It's always very difficult to play as there is no sound check, but if you can somehow forget about the monitors and get involved with the magic and energy of the crowd then it is amazing. We had production for the first time at a festival – i.e. a few of our own lights and a glitter drop for the last song!!!

'Think the best spectacle I have ever seen there was watching the Foo Fighters play the tent in the afternoon on their way up... I've never seen a crowd like it, ever... It was crowd surfing mania. There were probably two or three people coming over the barriers a second. I was a bit worried about safety at one point but it was so exiting at the same time that the exhilaration was phenomenal... strange thing was I'm not even a fan of Foo Fighters! When a band is in the ascendance it can really go that way and the reaction seemed to me to be as much about celebrating Nirvana again as welcoming back Dave Grohl!'
**Matt James (Gene – Drums)**

'We were headlining the tent and the Foo Fighters had played the night before, their debut UK show. It was just after 'Girl from Mars' had come out and there were so many people trying to get into the tent. There was some daring guy climbed up to the top of the tent pole and was just hanging there. It was just a really insane vibe, I couldn't believe it. Since then I've always known that the 'Reading Atmosphere' is really special. It's a real rock festival and the best for high energy music.'
**Tim Wheeler (Ash – Vocals/Guitar)**

'That morning, our tour bus was parked alongside all the other buses behind the stage and we would have been inside it, sleeping late, if it weren't for Green Day's 10am set. We had never heard of a band playing at 10:00 in the morning and wondered what would happen, so we got up and started walking around looking for Green Day. We found them eventually and they were great, of all things. Then I found my sister and her husband and killed the rest of the day with them, talking about everything BUT music. Suddenly, it was time to play. "This is gonna be fun," I thought. I walked up to the mic to start singing, placed my feet in the power stance that works best for screaming at the top of one's lungs, opened my mouth and not a sound came out. I stepped

Chris Cornell of Soundgarden during their only Reading performance

away from the mic, played another intro progression and tried again: nothing. I had no idea what sound I was supposed to be making, only a vague impression of words and notes mashed together to form lyrics which would, along with the music, make a song. '"Weird. Hope THAT never happens again," I thought, as I started the next song. As it turns out, those lyrics were missing, too, as were all the lyrics to every song on the set list, and, presumably, to every song I'd ever written. My husband, standing in the wings, looked like he was ready to call an ambulance. For an hour, I just walked around the stage, playing instrumentals and wondering what new kind of brain damage I had. When it was over, a journalist stopped me backstage and said, 'That was so... interesting. Most bands just play the songs the way they are on the record!"

'"That's what we were trying to do," I said. As it turned out, we got better reviews for that set than we had ever before.'
**Kristin Hersh (Throwing Muses – Vocals/Guitar)**

'My first ever experience was walking literally into the camps and an old woman coming up to me and saying "let's get pissed and grab some bollocks!!" and she came running over to me, a small 14 year old, and grabbed my bollocks as hard as she could. That was an interesting experience and I thoug I'll have to go back every year to see if I can get it again!!!'
**Tom Bellamy (The Cooper Temple Clause – Guitar/ Bass/Synthesizer/ Keyboard/ Trumpet/Programming/ Samples/Melodica/Percussion/Toy Piano/Bow/Decks/FX/ Beats/Vocals)**

'We were playing an all-new set with Kim playing bass for the first time and we were all a bit nervous. The crowds for the big stages scared me. We tried to stay backstage as much as possible. Kim remembers Booby Joe from Green Day spitting straight into the air, then catching it again in his mout Apparently, this had a disturbing effect on her since she still recalls it to this day.'
**Kreg Sterns (Nyack – Vocals/Guitar)**

**Bjork screams in the darkness**

'Our gig went well – the crowd was way into it. Some of my observations were that I remember Courtney looking so wasted that she practically tore apart the stage during Hole's set, and then wouldn't get off the stage.'
**Kim Collister (Nyack – Bass)**

'This was my first rock festival. I'd played Glastonbury, but the crowds there are largely fuelled by cannabis, which makes for a much mellower time than when you're faced with an alcohol-inspired Reading crowd, who are ready to destroy "That Which Does Not Satisfy". Thankfully, they liked me. To be honest, I was just glad to get out alive.'
**Bastard Son of Tommy Cooper (Magician)**

'The performance by the Smashing Pumpkins at the 1995 Festival was a turning point musically for me. They were on after Hole and Green Day, who I had seen many times and was really into at the time. But as they took the stage, it seemed the noise they produced made the bands before sound two-dimensional in comparison.'
**Som Wardner (My Vitriol – Vocals/Guitar)**

'We were founded in 1995, when Festival Welfare Services (FWS) sadly lost their government funding and had to pull out of the Reading Festival at the last minute. So I pulled together a team in just three weeks and off we went! All the team are great people and really dedicated to helping out people in need, while having some fun too. They are all professional people – general and psychiatric nurses, counsellors, social workers, youth workers and so on – and they work voluntarily, in exchange for a ticket.

'I still remember some of the people we helped out that first year. A couple of young women from Scandinavia were most surprised (and thankfully uninjured) when a flaming tin of beans shot through their tent, missing them by inches. Someone had been heating it without opening it first and it exploded and took out three tents. One young man had lost a single shoe. Rather than waste his beer money he opted to hop for the rest of the weekend – which he did too.

'We also find clean clothes for the poor souls who fall in the ditches or just get naked for some reason and forget what they've done with them! Or, as in the case of one man who took off his clothes, so they wouldn't get spoiled by the anti-climb paint when he scaled one of the marquees. He slipped, of course, and got covered in it. And that stuff doesn't want to come off! And it's not just people who come to us in need. In 2002 Jellybean the Chicken needed some assistance, as did a lost tabby cat the following year! One saucer of milk and she was on her way.'
**Corinne Lane (Reading Welfare Point Team Co-ordinator)**

111

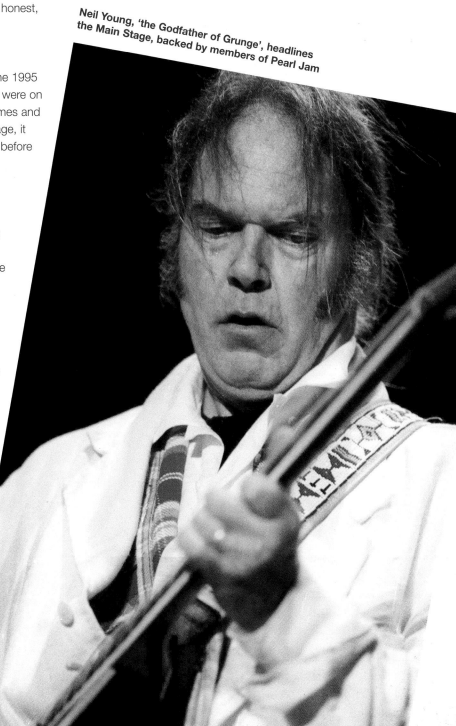

Neil Young, 'the Godfather of Grunge', headlines the Main Stage, backed by members of Pearl Jam

# 1996

Sunday proved to be more eventful for the Stone Roses than expected. With a band that sounded amazing, but a singer that sounded awful, this gig was their death knell and the end of their career as a band. There was an upsurge of 'American Punk' bands with Offspring, Weezer, Sebadoh and Garbage on the main stage and the Reading debut of both Placebo and Rocket From The Crypt in the tent. In the Doc Martens tent a small band played called Tripping Daisy, featuring Tim DeLaughter, who later went on to form Polyphonic Spree.

'When we played we had lots of fireworks during our show, the sun was going down and we played "Oh Yeah", which was a big hit that summer. And there were plenty of topless girls in the crowd, it was pretty wild! It was just insane to see that sea of people all jumping up and down to the same song.'
**Tim Wheeler (Ash – Vocals/Guitar)**

'This was our first major UK festival since debuting at number one with "1977", and I remember us all really feeling the pressure. I think we coped admirably with the heat and hysteria and rushed off to get liquored up for our heroes, Sonic Youth and the Stone Roses.'
**Rick McMurray (Ash – Drums)**

'I must admit that I now think we probably took our principle of not playing our best-known songs a bit too far. Mark E Smith had always inspired me. Whenever you saw The Fall, you knew that you were going to get a set full of material that you'd never heard before. And I really liked that. If you want to hear the old favourites… go play the old records! But I appreciate now that the festival crowd isn't your crowd, and that at least some effort should be made to accommodate people who aren't the hugest of fans. Apparently, after we'd played "Venus" from our new album *Saturnalia*, I said: "Britpop can shove that up its arse". Charming!'
**David Gedge (The Wedding Present – Vocals/Guitar)**

'One of The Prodigy crew at that time was Phil, who looked after Liam and (apparently) Gizz Butt who was The Prodigy guitarist between 1996 and 1999. Phil was initially paid to look after Liam and when Gizz came on board he was told he must look after Gizz too, but his wages did not rise with the extra responsibility. Not a penny more.

'This meant Phil would often neglect the guitar rig and hint to Gizz that maybe he should check things over himself. With this vague arrangement, the show was open to random events, with both sides trying to ignore what might happen. It was like trying to ignore the Black Death.

During the briefest of sound checks, Gizz stepped in front of 80,000 adoring fans to check his guitar. After striking an F sharp power chord repeatedly for 30 seconds, it was pretty obvious that there was no doubt the guitar was not coming through any monitors and was absolutely swamped by the overwhelming and gloriously loud on-stage sub frequencies of Liam's keyboard set up. Gizz tried to catch the attention of the monitor engineer: "Hey mate, there's no guitar coming through this rig." Another strum, a bent ear, and another shrugged shoulder.

'The Prodigy started their show in glorious technicolour and the crowd squirmed and shambled to get closer to their idols. Keith dragged his mic stand on stage as the opening sample to "Firestarter" was played. The big moment. The song of the hour. The most popular song in the world at that moment in time being played at the UK's most popular festival at that moment in time. And here comes Gizz's opening guitar chord, that grand, metallic F sharp power chord

'It was a big night, a loud night, a 75,000 crowd all looking at The Prodigy spectacle. All looking at Gizz about to play a silent guitar part. Where there should have been a CHANG!!! There was a squeak, where there should have been a RRRRRRRRRRRRRRRRR OOOOOOOOOOOOO RRRRRRRRRRR!!! There was a fart! Wiping the sweat off the back of his neck, Gizz spotted something dubious. A cable from the back of the Marshall guitar amp going to the monitor desk. There was a volume control next to the cable output. It was on ZERO. "What??? Is that why I can't hear myself??? Of course. It's a speaker simulator. It's supposed to be carrying the signal from my amplifier to the monitors but it's on zero. That's it!!! Simple remedy, I'll turn it up."

Gizz proceeded to crank up the volume three-quarters of the way up full. Little did he know he was loading the barrels of the world's loudest gun.... "NNNNNNNNNNNNNNNNNNNNNN NNNNNN EEEEEEEEEEEEEEEEEEEEEEEEEEEEEEEE YYYYY YYYYYYYYYYYYYYYYYYYYYYYYYYYYYYYY AAAAAAAAAA AAAAAAAAAAAAAAAAAAAAAAAAA NNNNNNNNNNNNNNN

The press conference before the ill-fated performance by the Stone Roses

Wrapped in plastic and sheltering from the rain

Festival favourite food...NOODLES

NNNNNNNNNNNNNNN GGGGGGGGGGGGGGGGGGGGGGGG
GGGGGGGGGGGGGGGGGGGGGGGGGGGGGGGGGGGGGGG!!!!!!"
The pressure pushed Keith Flint's hair back; everyone winced
in ear-splitting agony. For a second, which seemed like hours,
there was an atomic-bomb-being-detonated moment as
everyone was running in panic to turn down this guitar, which
was unleashing unquestionably the loudest guitar chord in the
world. AC/DC had nothing on this motherfucker.
The song ended. The crowd went mental. Back in the
dressing rooms, Liam wasn't happy. "I didn't touch it" said
Phil in defence, shifting the blame. "Gizz?" "Er, yeah, well, the
monitor man...." "Don't worry, he's just been sacked" said
John Fairs, saving Gizz's bacon. "Good let's fucking make sure
that doesn't happen again. Fucked up my ears forever, that
cunt" "Yeah, me too" said Gizz in relief, spotting suspicious
stares being thrown from Keith, as Phil vacated the room.'
**Gizz Butt (The Prodigy – Guitar)**

'I also witnessed the pivotal moment when the Stone Roses
headlined the event. History has painted it as a bleak day for
the Roses. I still say that if Ian's voice was lower in the mix,
it would have been a different story.'
**Clint Boon (Backstage Guest)**

'During The Stone Roses I remember crowd surfing and just
as I got near the pit, someone jostled me and my car keys fell
out of my pocket. I crawled around for 20 minutes between
people's legs, getting trodden on, but eventually found my
keys!! I managed to get out of there a wreck.'
**John Harper (The Cooper Temple Clause – Drums/
Gretsch Drums/DW Snares/ Sabian Cymbals/
Percussion/Backing Vocals)**

'Watching 10,000 people in '96 become
a muscular mass of limbs, sweat and love.'
**Martin Rossiter (Gene – Vocals)**

'Our dressing room was so full of people drinking and snorting
that I used Rage Against the Machine's portakabin next door
to get changed after the show. Only to have them walk back in
catching me in a state of undress! They were very nice about
it... I think pity and mirth overtook any RRRRRRage!!!'
**Leigh Marklew (Terrovision – Bass)**

'We got to the site a bit rough. I tried to take a shower in
one of the trailers... ended up getting about as muddy as I
started getting in and out of there... This opens a theme in my

114

perception of Reading as being one of the worst physical sites for a festival I can imagine… it always ends up looking like a Flemish field in 1916 and there's nowhere to hide from the dirt…. Anyhow, our set was pretty high energy; we stormed through most of what at that time was our latest album, *Amazing Disgrace*.'

**Ken Stringfellow (The Posies – Vocals/Guitar/Keyboards)**

'I remember the sea of people in the mid afternoon giving it up for us, that was a great feeling. To reach so many at once! People from all over the world gathered in one small place to witness the greatest bands of the times!'

**Christopher 'Krasp' Lee (Downset – Drums/ Rhythmic programmer)**

'The part of the human brain that deals with smell is well connected to our brain's memory banks and whenever one smells certain aromas one is instantly transported, time machine like, to that vivid scene. Damp straw, sweat, stale beer and smoke, in that order, can conjure me back to any Reading.'

**Kris Dweeb (Dweeb – Vocals/Guitar)**

'Me and two friends, Christine (who runs the world-famous Troubadour in Hollywood) and Jay traveled to Europe. Upon arriving in the UK, I started to notice the little differences that allow festivals to be a success there, but are just not feasible in America. The first and most obvious is the efficiency of the train system. On the day of the big festival, my friends and I took the train up to Reading, knowing that after we all got wasted, no one would have to drive home. Also, I remember a distinct feeling of camaraderie between everyone. We were all there together and for the same reason, which makes people feel safe, like we would all run in the same direction if disaster struck. It was all so foreign to me that at the

time, I was on sensory overload. But looking back, I, along with 80,000 other people, had an experience like no other. At that point in my life, I would have never thought that five years later, I would be standing on that same stage performing for 80,000.'

**John e. (OPM – Vocals)**

Julian Cope in a dress, 'nuff said?

# 1997

**The 'Mighty Metallica' stole the show on the Sunday, plundering their back catalogue and previewing tracks from *ReLoad*. Marilyn Manson appeared on the main stage for the first time and Bush appeared, with Gwen Stefani watching her husband to be (Gavin Rossdale) from the side of the stage. Super Furry Animals brought their large blue tank and the Lemonheads made their final Reading appearance.**

'We were added to the bill very late, so our name wasn't even on the backstage pass. It didn't matter to the band, though, we were very happy to be there at all. For me, it was a huge honour to be playing with two of my favorite bands, The Descendents and Metallica. I got to meet James Hetfield and we spoke about Ennio Morricone, my favorite soundtrack composer. Also there that day was Gwen Stefani, who was with her then boyfriend Gavin from Bush. She's so beautiful that no one forgets her!'
**Dave Neabore (Dog Eat Dog – Bass)**

'I think the Manics were headlining and I saw the Verve make their comeback in the tent, people were being pulled out without their legs broken!'
**Tom Smith (Editors – Vocals/Guitar)**

'I remember my first Reading, camping with mates and going down the front to see Stereophonics opening the main stage (a few years before they headlined). My favourite performance was the Boo Radleys in the first year I went. They headlined the second stage, and I've still got the drumstick. Also Mastodon last year.'
**Huw Stephens (Main Stage Compere)**

**Building the framework for the Main Stage**

**Fountains of Wayne**

View from above

raise the battered punk rock standard, sweat like a wild feral beast and then piss off and hang out and watch loads of bands whilst other bands moan about being outside and fuck off back to the hotel.'
**John Robb (Goldblade – Vocals/Guitar)**

'My fondest memory was when I befriended my childhood hero Milo Auckerman, lead singer of American punk legends The Descendents. The Descendents had soundtracked my youth and coincidentally Dweeb

'I'm at a medieval freak show, gurning twisted faces scorched by the fierce August sun, fly infested mud mashed in with rubbish crusts its way along the pathways, tents stretch into the distance whilst the usual English grey rain clouds gang up in the distance. The children of middle England are all stoned, pissed, smashed and merry and somewhere in the distance there is the dull thud of the bass drum pulling us in to main arena.

'Fuck, it's Reading and another summer is over! Back down to the three-day bacchanal by the Thames. Celebrate the filth and the noise! For the sheer number of bands that you actually like, then Reading always gets the vote. An endless stream of noisy guitar guerrillas interspersed with lame indie ducks and rubbish flavour of the month fashion saps too scared to get their kecks muddy when they step out of the tour bus that they will only be able to afford for one year, it's a conveyer belt of pasty faced hopefuls and some genius rock action. It's more hit than miss and I've seen some great stuff there over the years, as well playing there twice with Goldblade which was fantastic – a packed tent with a crowd going wild, you could see the steam pouring off people; we thought we would be booked to play there forever after that! Instead we have to make do with the festivals all over the world, enjoying the no sound check get-up-and-play rush, hit the boards, storm the stage, celebrate the noise, grab the mic and dive headlong into the moshpit… ! The consummate festival band, rip it up,

had been encoring with the Descendents classic "Silly Girl". I spied him sitting alone in the catering tent contemplating a plate of festival fodder. I sat down next to him and struck up a conversation I will never forget. The Descendents were on the main stage in an hour. After grilling him and explaining what joy his band had brought to my life, I invited him to join us for the encore of "Silly Girl" that we were to perform that night.

'Seven o'clock came round and Milo turned up to our trailer sipping a beer and watched our entire set from behind the curtain until it was his cue to join us. Never in a million years, if anyone had told me before that I would be on stage at Reading singing this great song with Milo in front of a packed festival tent going nuts, would I ever had believed them! And to boot the gent was the nicest, most unassuming, self-effacing humble soul you could ever hope to meet. I still don't know if he realises how much his music has crept around the globe and continues to bring such joy to millions.'
**Kris Dweeb (Dweeb – Vocals/Guitar)**

'My experience is limited to the traffic chaos caused when I visit locations in Reading around festival time. I avoid driving if at all possible around the weekend.'
**John Holden (Book Sanctuary – Reading)**

# 1998

They weren't Led Zeppelin, but they played their songs. Page and Plant headlined in what was as close to a Led Zep reunion as you would ever get. This year the Phoenix Festival was cancelled and many of the bands were added to the Reading bill. There was an ongoing argument between Beastie Boys and the Prodigy about the latter's song 'Smack My Bitch Up' which the Beasties did not want them to perform, as it was demeaning to women. This was coming from the Beastie Boys, whose first UK tour saw women in cages and giant penises onstage.

'We did it just before the *Nuclear Sounds* album came out and we played second from the top, just below Page and Plant. We had these cool pyros during the song "Numbskull" and we had to stand ten feet back, because when they went off we were "bricking it"!! It was the only time that we had played the main stage in the dark.'
**Tim Wheeler (Ash – Vocals/Guitar)**

'Being forgiven for cancelling in '98 and having the reason, my daughter Evie's birth, announced on stage.'
**Martin Rossiter (Gene – Vocals)**

'I remember Lee Perry turning up 30 minutes before he was due to go on without any equipment and him having to use ours, even down to one of us (Sanjay) doing his out front sound. What an honour! We were on straight after and all I remember is Money Mark, without his pass, trying to get on stage with us and miraculously seeing off scores of bouncers without lifting a finger, strolling casually onstage saying "hi" and then walking off pursued by exasperated bouncers. Reading, rock and real ale forever!'
**Steve Chandrasonic Savale
(Asian Dub Foundation – Guitar)**

'I know I took a few Es and when it came to the gig I was ready for anything and was jumping about like a goblin at an Irish wake. It felt like our role was to be that year's Hawkwind; we did that by sounding like the Blockheads in a wind tunnel. I tried my hand at dancing and that's not something I do lightly. I was thinking as I was doing it that the crew should really kit me out with one of them wraparound mics that Madonna uses, as it was getting difficult to sing and dance at the same

time. The Es helped me with the dancing but my jokes were rubbish and few pints always work best for gags. The crowd seemed to love it, I know I did. On my death bed I think it will flash before my eyes as a moment where I really had the world by my own balls for once or something.'
**Paul Vickers (Dawn of the Replicants – Vocals)**

'On a train going to the Reading Festival to DJ in a dance tent… weird. Do Reading "do" dance, one of my guests asked. "Dunno" was my reply, "but we're about to find out!"

'Alongside me on the line-up was Bentley Rhythm Ace, Deejay Punk Roc, Monkey Mafia, Justin Robertson, The Lo-Fidelity Allstars (DJ'ing), Les Rhythm Digitales (Local Reading boy… now superstar producer to Madonna!!) and DJ Touche. Basically it was our Big Beat Boutique gang! Descending on Reading with our own brand of "dance music". Skint had just blown up big time, thanks to the successful Big Beat Boutique nights we were doing and also the talents of a certain Fat Boy Slim!

'I'll be honest with you… with the heady mix of Carlsberg lager, vodka and partying hard I don't think many of us truly remember to its full extent the day, but I remember having a great time… playing a great set… to a great tent full of punters on a beautiful sunny Sunday! The great thing is I think we were the first people to grace Reading Festival with the dance music Arena, and we were such a success that they have been doing it ever since!"
**Cut La Roc (DJ/Scratch-Mix Specialist)**

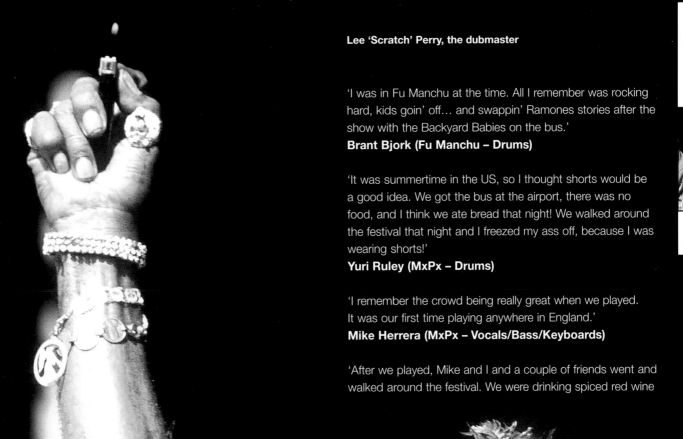

**Lee 'Scratch' Perry, the dubmaster**

'I was in Fu Manchu at the time. All I remember was rocking hard, kids goin' off… and swappin' Ramones stories after the show with the Backyard Babies on the bus.'
**Brant Bjork (Fu Manchu – Drums)**

'It was summertime in the US, so I thought shorts would be a good idea. We got the bus at the airport, there was no food, and I think we ate bread that night! We walked around the festival that night and I freezed my ass off, because I was wearing shorts!'
**Yuri Ruley (MxPx – Drums)**

'I remember the crowd being really great when we played. It was our first time playing anywhere in England.'
**Mike Herrera (MxPx – Vocals/Bass/Keyboards)**

'After we played, Mike and I and a couple of friends went and walked around the festival. We were drinking spiced red wine

Disco Pistol, local band from Reading

and checking everything out. We have festivals in America, but nothing like this.'
**Tom Wisniewski (MxPx – Guitar)**

'Check the day sheet paper to see where the hell I am and realize that it's Reading and there are tons of bands I want to see, so it would be good to be clean. I don't know why it's important to be clean when seeing music, but regardless, I wake Karina up and we grab our train cases and head out of the bus, wrapped in towels, rat's nest hair, looking a straight half-naked WRECK.

'It's a tricky endeavor, looking for an elusive festival shower while trying to be totally stealthy to make sure no one sees you. We diligently set off across the field, walking quickly so as not to be detected by all of the crew guys getting the stages set up. Should have checked the day sheet to see what time doors opened, because as we were halfway across the field, gates opened and we were suddenly run down by a THUNDERING HERD of festival goers. Karina and I couldn't keep our towels up and run fast enough to evade the herd.

**ABOVE: The Beastie Boys**

Plus we were laughing too hard.'
**Elyse Rogers (Dance Hall Crashers – Vocals)**

'I do remember how huge that festival was, and thinking this must take a long time to plan, because the place is just crawling with things to see, many stages, and people from all over Europe. That was also the first time I ever saw or heard of that little band called Muse.'
**Rory Koff (No Use For A Name – Drums)**

'We were the first band on the *Melody Maker* stage on the Friday. It was amazing to be asked to play Reading once, we were amazed when they asked us back. We all felt like kids in a sweety shop. We still feel really lucky to have been there... Reading rocks....'
**Hyper Helen (Disco Pistol – Keyboards)**

'It's the first time you get to earn some real money! The fee might have been something like a £1000.00 or something,

which seemed colossal to us! It's the first time the fee doesn't disappear into fags and petrol money. When the adverts come out, it's always a good time to assess your worth in the eyes of the music industry, by seeing who's above and below you on the bill.'
**Darren Hayman (Hefner – Vocals/Guitar)**

'Anyway, we load up the Renault Extra with beer and a few Milletts tents and set off for Reading. We are told we can camp in the guest area. This VIP field has its own plastic chemical toilets, but these are already a death-trap by the time we reach there. We set up camp. It's hot, we're bending all our tent pegs in the rock-hard ground, and the beers are warming up, so we think it wise to drink them before they get undrinkable. We are not playing till noon the next day, so there's no pressure.

'The following day we get ready to play the gig. Some of our "equipment" was not just unreliable, but complete rubbish. Back then we didn't use bass much but when we did, Dunc used to switch from guitar to bass. We had a decent bass

**ABOVE: Festival of the long shadows**

Marshall 4X12, but no proper guitar cab for him, so he was using an ancient Vox stack that belonged to me. It didn't stand up properly, so we used to lay it on its side on top of the 4X12, thereby giving a kind of "Stonehenge" look that we thought was funny but sounded shit.

'We sat around for what seemed like hours in our allocated portakabin, adjusting bow ties and wondering if it was worth changing six-month-old guitar strings, and naturally, drinking. This may have had some effect on our performance. About three songs in I remember thinking, how come I can't hear either Dunc's guitar or Jonny's Keyboards? It was revealed to us later that Dunc's was plugged into the DI box but not his guitar amp, and Jonny's amp was not even switched on!!

'So far so good. I do remember seeing Page and Plant. They did a lot of Zep faves and appeared to have a wind machine blowing back the singer's hair.'
**Chris Teckkam (Ten Benson – Vocals/Guitar)**

# 1999

The Chili Peppers were back for their second headline performance and Blur proved that they were one of the longest-lasting Brit Pop bands. The second leg of the festival was introduced this year, at Temple Newsam in Leeds. The bands would play Reading and then Leeds the next day, so the Sunday bands would play on Bank Holiday Monday. This would change eventually, with bands playing different days of the weekend.

'The beginning of the show was disorganised and frantic. At that time, Cinerama used considerably more equipment than the Wedding Present, with samplers, keyboards and a flute player added to our traditional guitars, bass and drums. Unfortunately, the festival technicians had been sent a copy of the wrong stage plan and channel list and, somewhat inevitably, chaos ensued. Stage times at events like these are non-negotiable, however. In fact, I believe bands are fined for overrunning their slot because they've started late, so despite a sophisticated 'going-onstage' strategy worked out by our sound engineer Suneil Pusari, we ended up beginning our set before he was ready for us. The concert itself was great, though. Cinerama was not as well-known as the Wedding Present, so the audience was almost exclusively composed of hardcore fans. The crowd's reaction was tremendous, but I fear that Cinerama was neither trendy nor commercially successful enough to be invited back.'
**David Gedge (Cinerama – Vocals/Guitar)**

'It was quite a thrill to play Reading the first time on Steve Lamaq's Radio One stage.'
**Jimi Goodwin (Doves – Vocals/Bass/Guitar/Drums)**

'One thing I really remember from that show was that I had a couple of extra passes and I went out into the crowd and I ran into these two kids who were 11 and 12 years old and they couldn't believe that I was just walking around in the crowd. I was like "here, take these passes, you can go backstage and they just freaked out. I guess it made their lives at that point. They were backstage hanging out with the Offspring, Chili Peppers and Sporty Spice!'
**Pete Koller (Sick Of It All – Guitar)**

'We played the main stage and it was pretty awesome as we started doing the "Braveheart", which we've made into one of our official show things. It was a pretty awesome moment, because up until then we had only done it at club shows, so to step out onto the stage at Reading and to have all the crowd doing it with the big line going back to the soundboard, it was incredible.'
**Lou Koller (Sick Of It All – Vocals)**

'When it was time to go on the lads went up first and started, then I went up. What a bang, the place went mental, people flying all over the place. It just felt amazing. All of us were somewhere else, the music seemed to be playing itself. I'll never forget that gig. It was one of the best I've ever felt, the crowd was amazing, you just wanted to be part of them. It all seemed to end very quickly, like a blur or something. Mind you, could have been all the beer and the doobie. We left the stage rushing, kind of like after doing a bungee or something.'
**Declan O'Shea (Cyclefly – Vocals)**

'Earlier that year we had our biggest and worst hit, "Tequila", and had been dropped by EMI. So we played third top on the bill, below the Chili Peppers and Offspring, as an unsigned band!! We introduced a new song to the crowd for the first time called "Friends and Family", and by all accounts the chorus "Party over here, fuck you over there" was the looped singalong all that night in the campsites. During the first song we had a very original crowd surfer... who was passed over the heads of the moshpit whilst fully reclined in a bath tub reading a newspaper.'
**Leigh Marklew (Terrorvision – Bass)**

'It felt like a huge wake-up call to arms. That atmosphere of Y2K and the fact that the century ended that year created a certain intensity. Many people thought the world could end a few months later. When Nic Endo started her earthquake noise intro and the girl singer Hanin Elias did that famous scream "The Time Is Right To Fiiiiigggghhhht!" I looked at the horizon; it was such great scenery. The massive crowd, the cloudy sky, thousands of fists.'
**Alec Empire (Atari Teenage Riot – Programming/Shouts)**

'I woke up late on the bus and was very hung-over and wanted to take a shower. After much wandering I stumbled to an outdoor port-o-potty type shower. After taking my clothes off and getting in, I stood under a freezing trickle of reclaimed water and screamed and shivered. At this point I realized I'd brought no towel, no soap, no razor and no change of clothes. I walked back to the bus, wet and freezing in my dirty

Blur's Damon Albarn

Beer! Crates of the stuff on the way to the campsite

clothes, and thought that most of the people who attend the festival assume that the artists lead a glamorous and dignified lifestyle.... This is not always true... I'm proof.... A couple of hours later we performed in the tent and I hung my naked unclean body from the support poles to entertain the lovely music fans that really know how to rough it....'"

**Warren Anthony Fitzgerald (The Vandals – Guitar/Vocals)**

'All four members of Lit unanimously agree that the 1999 Reading Festival has been the largest and best show in our 15-year history. Surrounded by mud and wounded by booze, we tumbled out of the bus and staggered around to the backstage area, looking for anything to help us with our hangovers. I remember going up on the stage around 11:00 am and looking out at the empty muddy field.  It looked huge... no, massive. After changing clothes and powering down some much needed water, we approached the ramp and prepared to hit the Reading stage.

'I took a casual peek out at the audience and I was entirely blown away by how many people had shown up in just an hour's time. It was so jammed, the crowd just seemed to get blurry in the far back and we couldn't even tell where the sea of people ended. At high noon, we stepped onstage (still hung over) and played – what we call to this day – the biggest show of our lives. The official crowd estimate was around 60,000 plus people. We were eventually told by a long-time festival staff member, that this was the largest crowd he'd ever seen gather for an opening band.'

**Kevin Baldes (Lit – Bass)**

'Back at the Reading Festival the entire band and crew were amped. It was the first time we'd ever hit the main stage, so we were all a little crazy. I remember getting up there and seeing 50,000+ people going nuts to "Genius" and "Microwaved" and all the Pitchshifter tracks we pulled out that day. Our time slot flew by way too fast and all of a sudden we were done. The crowd were exhausted, the band were on cloud nine. Leaving the stage we had our entire entourage with us. Main stage at Reading is a big deal and everyone and their dog wanted to be a part of it. I did tell them all that the band weren't all that famous or influential and that we didn't have any rock-star friends back stage, but they didn't believe me and showed up in hope of stumbling across Brad Pitt doing a rail off of The Corrs' asses anyway. Suddenly I heard a loud voice calling me from behind as we all walked to the dressing room. The voice was loud enough to silence our entire entourage.

'"So what's up, you don't hang with yo' friends no more?". It was Ice-Muthafukkin'T. He walked over to me and gave me a peace hug to the amazement of my friends. "You know Ice-T?"

'"Yeah, you know how it is. Me and Ice are tight. At that point my cell-phone rang. It was Pitchshifter's tour manager. "I don't know what the hell you think you're doing, but you have a live Radio One interview in five minutes backstage."

'The fucking horror. Back in those days we'd sneakily do a "hit" on stage before the last song, so that we were flying by the time we hit the dressing room. Those hits were kicking in like a pair of angry mules. We were both lit-up like cheap plastic Christmas trees, and we only had five minutes to traverse the entire crowd and address the nation. Needless to say, we arrived a little late, told them to play some Pink Floyd and dribbled gibberish in to the mic (to the abject horror of our management). You gotta love Reading.'

**J S Clayden (Pitchshifter – Vocals/Programming)**

'Oddly enough, the very first My Ruin show was the Reading Festival. My most memorable moment of the show was walking on stage and having all sorts of dolls that were decorated to look like me thrown up on the stage from the crowd. It was very strange. Our crew picked them up and I ended up attaching them and a few heads and bodies which had come apart to my mic stand after the show and proceeded to add more and more nightly as we started our first UK tour. I also remember this show as being one of the most electric nights I ever felt on stage and the crowd was beautifully brutal. It was like a drug. It was quite a night of rock 'n' ruin....on many levels.'

**Tarrie B (My Ruin – Vocals)**

'We didn't have the right passes to get on the main stage but managed to get up there to watch Sick Of It All kill it. So, same predicament later when the Chili Peppers went on, but this time we snuck up the side of the stage and sat down at the front of the stage on Flea's side about ten feet to the right of where he was standing... yet out of the way of the view of security. We videotaped their whole set... a few times Flea would look over at us filming and all we could do was smile back! Watching the Red Hot Chili Peppers playing in front of 60,000 people from the stage, directly across from Rick Rubin... amazing experience!!!'

**Brett Rasmussen (Ignite – Bass)**

'Usually we are sandwiched between the main stage and the *NME* stage or new band stage, or something like that. It can, if you hit the wrong slot, be one of the worst gigs a comedian can have. You don't get bottles of piss thrown at you but you do start to wonder if you are, or indeed ever have been, funny. Of course there have been some great gigs there, in fact there was one that the booking agent still swears is the best gig he's ever seen me do anywhere, ever. The one that sticks in my head was when I took to the stage and, what with it being a young crowd, asked if they'd ever seen pubic hair and then got me cock out, only to look down and see my eight-year-old son with his nose pressed to the barrier. I thought I'd told him to stay backstage. Bet he was proud of his Dad.'
**Ian Cognito (Comedian)**

'People always talk about the "Festival Spirit", but I never really understood what the hell it was all about, and I had no frame of reference.... Maybe it was because I was a young kid and

my first experience of seeing 100,000 people singing along to Blur playing "This Is A Low", it was just unbelievable and amazing.'
**Alex White (The Electric Soft Parade – Vocals/Guitar/keyboards)**

'I got my credentials and a map and decided to have a walk in the rain to inspect the goings on.... When we came out to play, we really didn't know what to expect, or even if people were going to come see us. Our show rocked and we were greeted by one of the loveliest crowds we've ever played to. These kids can rock.'
**Chris Burney (Bowling For Soup – Guitar)**

'We'd never been overseas and didn't know what the Reading Festival was! We didn't really know what we were getting into. When we arrived, there were like 50,000 people.... We had a blast playing the show; there were about 2,000 kids in there, and it went really well for our first gig in the UK.'
**Gary Wiseman (Bowling For Soup – Drums)**

**A very quiet arena**

# 2000

**The festival debut of Oasis was marked with the most amazing 'electric lightshow' as a thunderstorm raged in the distance, with forked lightning adding to the effect and brightening up the arena. On the Sunday, Daphne & Celeste were pelted with anything the crowd could find during their three-song set and Slipknot proved that metal was alive and kicking in Iowa.**

'Reading was one of the best festivals we've ever played, and the thunder and lightning came right on queue!'
**Gem Archer (Oasis – Guitar)**

'The first time I saw Badly Drawn Boy, I just remember this bearded guy with a tea cosy on his head. He sang a song called "Pissing in The Wind." His set had been quite shambolic, but really moving. Near the end of the song, he took his harmonica and jumped down into the crowd. I was at the front and found the whole thing really inspiring. Speaking to him after I'd told him how his "warts and all" attitude had been really touching.

'Later, when we headlined the second stage, the tent was so full that they had to tear the sides off. I remember dedicating a song to everyone who was stood outside, and the cheer from out there was almost as loud as the cheer from inside. When we walked off I got a warning that we were almost over our time and that we would be fined if we carried on playing to the tune of £1000.00 a minute. Damon from Badly Drawn Boy was at the side of the stage with a big cheesy grin on his face. I don't know what hit me but I asked him if he wanted to come onstage and sing a song. I don't think he'd ever heard the song we were about to do, but I knew that wouldn't matter. When we both walked out the cheer was really loud. He said he was only doing it because it would look cool in the papers... the crowd laughed, and we were away.

'He shuffled around stage, found a guitar and started strumming along, joining in on vocals in the chorus to the song, which was a song off our first album called "One Big Family". I'm sure if someone played you a tape of the night it would be a mess... but the spirit of it made the day for me. Afterwards I nicked his hat. And we never did get fined.'
**Danny McNamara (Embrace – Vocals)**

'I always wanted to go, even for an American it's a well-known festival and great bands play every year. Primal Scream was a fucking amazing show and is still one of the best live shows I have ever seen. I watched bands in the tent and walked back

and forth to the main stage, and it was the only time that I ever fantasised about playing anywhere. When I was here, we'd just finished the record and I thought God this would be so  perfect, to be up there playing "Spread Your Love"... because it would just feel like the perfect festival anthem, with everyone singing and clapping their hands. I could picture it so perfectly in my mind. I was standing in the back of the tent and watching some band and picturing us up there and then two years later we were there headlining the tent.'
**Robert Turner (Black Rebel Motorcycle Club – Bass/Vocals)**

'Ian Brown popped into my portakabin to say "hi!" We performed "This Is How It Feels" to celebrate the fact that it was ten years to the day since the Inspirals' headline set.'
**Clint Boon (The Clint Boon Experience – Vocals/Keyboards)**

'I remember waking up in the grass and how surreal the whole thing felt. I vividly remember leaving the festival in a proper bus, going down a half lane road and barely missing the bodies. We eventually found our way to the main road and thankfully no one got hurt in the process. I remember seeing Rage Against The Machine and thinking to myself that they were one of the greatest bands of all time. I remember going on stage with the intention of just blowing every other band off the stage. We felt a lot of pressure, we stepped up to the plate and we owned it.'
**Clown #6 (Slipknot – Custom Percussion/Backing vocals)**

'The cool thing about us playing at the Reading Festival was we had played this show in Austin, Texas called "South X Southwest". Someone, who at that point was working for Mean Fiddler, saw us play the show. They sent us a random email saying "come play the festival", I had no idea what it was!! Our manager checked the website and it was like "this is a pretty big deal! We're gonna roll the dice and we're going to try to go over and do it!"

"We went over on our own money and played the side stage. I guess Radio One had played the "Bitch Song" and our cover of "Summer of '69" a few times. When we went on we were

The Gallagher brothers only appearance
– Oasis weather the storm

Deftones lead singer Chino Moreno

Slipknot conquer 'Metal Sunday'

on the smallest stage, but there were people as far as you could see, like out of the tent! It was insane!'
**Jaret Reddick (Bowling For Soup – Vocals/Guitar)**

'We got there and it was great and glorious, because we were at one of the coolest music festivals that we had all read about for years, and now we were playing at it. The album had come out the same week and we were walking through the crowd. We hadn't been there ten minutes and someone grabbed me by the shoulder and said "You're Bowling For Soup, aren't you? I bought your album two days ago and I recognised you from the picture inside!' That was an extremely fucked up situation, and really cool, that someone had recognised me.'
**Erik Chandler (Bowling For Soup – Bass)**

'My favourite performance at Reading was Primal Scream, at around the time of "Exterminator". They came onstage to "Swastika Eyes" and I was somewhat under the influence and it was breathtaking.'
**Daniel Fisher (The Cooper Temple Clause – Guitar/Bass/Vocals)**

'I think the best ever show I've seen... was at the Reading Festival, when Soulwax played the second stage.'
**Ben Gautrey (The Cooper Temple Clause – Guitar/Bass/Keyboards /Vocals)**

'As for playing the Reading Festival, we started out the first year in the Carling tent and it was fucking bonkers!!! We were in one of the backstage trailers and we heard this distant noise and tribal rumblings of a sort which, as we neared the stage, turned out to be people chanting for Amen ten minutes before we were even to hit the stage. I'm not good with numbers, but the stage was basically being ripped apart so that people could see the band from outside the tent. People were sitting on top of each other's shoulders, trying to see the band. I'll never forget the first time we played Reading, and to this day it remains one of the most important gigs, if not the most important, I've ever played.'
**Casey Chaos (Amen – Vocals)**

'We got lost on the way there, started to panic – as we were running late – and then the van got bumped into at the roundabout, just outside the festival site by a 17-year-old festival goer who had just passed her test. Panic levels rose as we stood at the roundabout exchanging addresses and getting very jumpy.

'Got to the backstage area in perfect time to unload the gear straight onto the stage. Got on stage and our drum machine was broken, so our drummer had to ad lib (to great effect) and we played a blinder. It was actually a very special gig, we went down really well – the pre gig stress got translated into stage magic.'
**Jo Bartlett (It's Jo and Danny – Vocals)**

'My first Reading was the year the Oasis pantomime took place on the main stage. After a troubled year, Noel and Liam managed to make it though their set but only with a serious amount of silly nonsense that would have been better sorted out backstage. The pair of them bickered and argued like brothers do, only these brothers chose to do it in front of 60,000 people. I remember seeing Primal Scream live for the first time.... Brilliant lasers accompanied the high energy set. Bobby and the boys in roaring form.'
**Chris Hawkins (Radio 6 DJ)**

'We were playing at the same time as Slipknot, so we were worried about the crowd, but luckily it pissed down, so they all came into the tent and it was amazing. At the end I started smashing my guitar up and I started smashing it over my head, and eventually I knocked myself out. I had a bit of the scratch plate stuck in my head and I had to go to hospital to get it removed. I turned up at hospitality again at about 9pm, with a big bandage around my head, and just got absolutely fuckin' shitfaced!! Just because we'd taken full advantage of the slot, worthy of the Crocketts, and tore it apart.'
**Davey MacManus (The Crocketts – Vocals/Guitar)**

'Some big stage bruiser pulled the plug on me after three songs, to make up for mismanaged time they had lost during the day. I think he may have thought "wee blonde thing" and it fixed their fuck up of running 45 minutes later than advertised in an instant. I had a few labels down to see me with a view to signing me. It was a total disaster. I was gutted. Thank God the memory of the Reading experience was changed for me for ever after that initial fateful show. The other shows were amazing.'
**Dot Allison (Dot Allison –Vocals/Piano/Guitar/Mandolin/Harmonica)**

'Oasis were incredible. They played during a thunderstorm and we were in the perfect place, where we stood, to see and hear them playing; every now and then fork lightning was striking the ground, in the distance, either side of the stage. It was an amazing natural light show.'
**Mike Horton (Festival Regular and Driver)**

'Priority on security is to salvage, hide and protect loo rolls, as they become scarce. Security are normally confined to sleeping in caravans (although 20-hour days are to be expected) and not the usual comfortable eight-man, more a 'Father Ted' style caravan, shared between ten or more of you! I have battled and made good friends, some of which I only met when escorting them out of the pit at the stage front. Believe it or not, depending who you work for, the money varies. But for the hours worked it's not that good. Most boys do it for the love of the festival.'
**Ade Dowrick (Security)**

'The volunteers at the Reading Welfare Point provide a wonderful service to the festival fans. Creating a safety net for those who fall outside the provided medical and security services.'
**Terri (Reading Festival Welfare Point)**

**LEFT: Stereophonics headline the Main Stage**

**BELOW: Dinner time for the seagulls**

# 2001

**Rap started and ended the festival with Run DMC on Friday afternoon and Eminem closing proceedings on Sunday night. Eminem also performed a duet with Marilyn Manson on the song 'The Way I Am', which would never have happened in the USA. Sunday was a mostly rock day, with Marilyn Manson, Queens of the Stone Age, Papa Roach, System of a Down and the return to the UK of the Cult.**

'With memories of the 1995 chaos still lingering in the memory, we are asked if we want to move to the main stage, but we take our chances, as we want to have headlined some part of Reading at some point in our career! It's the last festival for us in a summer packed with 40 festival appearances, and probably the high point gig-wise on the whole "Free All Angels" tour. Although no fatalities occur, judging by the crush at the front it was a close run thing. We even heard after the show that there were a few thousand people who didn't even make it into the tent, swarming outside attempting to catch a glimpse!'
**Rick McMurray (Ash – Drums)**

'They had me on in the Dance Tent, which I was really nervous about. I was absolutely shitting my pants to be honest, it was the most nervous I'd been before a gig since I was 18 and doing my first gig in a pub. Absolutely terrified. It just seemed the completely wrong place for me to be and it was disappointing to be there and not on one of the bigger stages. I couldn't talk for about two hours before we went on, I was so frightened. Which isn't like me, as I don't get stage fright normally. But it was brilliant as it turned out and other people came in from elsewhere. It went really well. My memories of it post-gig are fantastic. I had a really good time and it was a lovely atmosphere and a good selection of bands.... But prior to it, I was cursing the very name of it!'
**Gary Numan (Gary Numan – Vocals)**

'My only memories of Reading are of working my way through the mud in stilettos and always being extremely overdressed! I'm not sure that I am the right person to speak of it, I'm just the fiancé [of Marilyn Manson] after all, just there to be supportive and wear high heels at all costs for him!'
**Dita Von Teese (Fetish Icon)**

'We were originally scheduled to be on the Carling stage, second on, but as we got closer, there was a bit of a vibe going on and we got moved up to one from top. We didn't really expect anything and we went on and it was insane! Then halfway through the set we heard a clinking, going "clink clink clink", and we thought it was someone testing something or

hitting a drum. Then we realised at the end of the song, that it was people trying to rebuild the barriers because they'd collapsed while we were playing! So we had to stop and wait, while they built the barriers back up. That changed a lot for us, because at Reading you have all the media there and so we had all these magazines and TV media people, thinking "Who the fuck is this band? Why the fuck are all these people here to see this band? We've never heard of them, they've never been in our magazine and we never hyped them." I'm not sure that many people can pinpoint the moment where people suddenly opened their eyes and started taking notice of you, but for us Reading was that moment.'
**Ian Watkins (Lostprophets – Vocals)**

Nick Oliveri performs naked in the rain with Queens of the Stone Age

**Relaxing at the festival
– What better way to
watch music?**

'You could play to a bigger crowd, but you would never get the reaction. I remember standing backstage and our banner went up and there was a big cheer. I was standing on the edge of the stage with my guitar and it was possibly the most nervous I had ever been going on stage, not knowing which way it was going to go. We played the first song and I had a few guitar problems. Reading is just about the music. Reading is awesome.'
**Mike Lewis (Lostprophets – Guitar)**

'I remember when we were kids growing up in sunny Scotland and the Reading Festival was this sacred event that all our favourite bands would come and play. I don't think we even knew where Reading was, but we knew that one day we'd very much like to be a part of it. Fast-forward several years, to us and several hairy Scotsmen fighting for sleeping space on the floor of a dodgy old van. Yes, we were going to the Reading Festival! I can recall waking with a very sore neck, but also a flutter in my heart when we realised we were actually at the Reading Festival.'
**James Johnston (Biffy Clyro – Bass/Vocals)**

'I'll never forget when a security guard came up to me and said "We're ready for ya this year! Rumour had it that you guys were the most violent band Reading had seen for quite a while! So we beefed up our security a couple times over." He shook my hand and laughed, saying "Have a great show." As for the crowd reaction, I don't think you could say anything but simply the best audience in the world. Open minded people going for the weekend with their friends to have a good fuckin' time with a great line up for a sonic backdrop. At the time Iggy Pop's son was tour managing the band and asked if I would be at the main stage to watch this one-hit-wonder type band, or at least be there for a few minutes because Jim (his Dad) was coming out with his lady. So I said "of course, I'll wait right here". Iggy said to me,"Alright Casey, let's see what all this hubbub is about." And like the king that he is, he watched a couple songs and patted me on the shoulder and said "Just what I thought." And went off into the sunset.
**Casey Chaos (Amen – Vocals)**

'It rained all weekend and was full of metal acts, which is really not my thing at all. I remember going into my bunk on the tour bus saying to everyone, "I'm going for a kip and when I awake the sun will be out and Otis Redding will be headlining the main stage!"'
**Kevin Miles (Gene – Bass)**

'So there we were; five slightly bedraggled young chaps strolling into the searing heat of the miniature new bands tent, determined to prove to the assorted masses on and offstage that we meant business. The half hour that proceeded was quite a blur; the photographic evidence of the day seemed to suggest that the din we made was equally matched by some loud shirts and even louder shorts.'
**Joe Birch (Hell is For Heroes – Drums)**

'I'd never been to a festival before that summer (you can take the boy out of Mull...). Anyhow, I remember waking up early and walking across the as-yet-empty site, across the fields, smelling the stalls, trying on some terrible hats, thinking I was cool!, while people were still turning in their sleeping bags in the tents. I was with Fab, the Strokes drummer, and we were like kids – especially him, as we walked right up to the punters' side of the barrier at the front of the empty main stage. He couldn't quite believe he was going to be standing up there on the other side in eight or so hours' time. It had all happened so fast for me I felt, let alone them! My favourite experience was the feeling of camaraderie among us all. Nick Valensi, their guitarist, acted as my guitar tech during my set because he was so nervous about playing later – he wanted to take his mind off it all. I remember him being a bit slow with the guitar changes! I still owe him a fee come to think of it. It was a great show. Full tent – it just felt really cool to be a part of this historic festival. I did buy that hat.'
**Colin MacIntyre (Mull Historical Society – Vocals/Guitar)**

'Me and the crew were all pretty bored backstage making fun of all the "try hard, wannabe" PR girls running around in their high heels trying to appear high and mighty in case anyone from the record company spotted them. Then all of a sudden we hear a rock version of Michael Jackson's "Smooth Operator" blast out over the speakers, me and Blade look at each other with that puzzled "who the fuck ever does Jacko cover versions?" look on our faces and we rush to the stage to check it out. Then a month later Alien Ant Farm was worldwide with the song... Puuure irony!!'
**Mark B (Mark B & Blade – Producer)**

'Reading was gonna be the last show before we called it a day and got some time off from all the travelling which took more out of us than the performances did. It is an artist's dream to be on the stage there, but the double whammy was that we also happened to be on the Radio One stage with some huge names, which was also a blessing for me and the crew. We got there the night before and wandered around the place and just soaked in the atmosphere and got to meet loads of cool people.

'The whole atmosphere was dynamic. We were on after Alien Ant Farm, so we knew we had to give it everything we had, which we did. The whole vibe from start to finish was electric. At one point I stage-dived into the crowd and crowd surfed until one punter decided to put me on his shoulders and carry me around the tent we were performing in. This I will never forget!!'
**Blade (Mark B & Blade – Vocals)**

'We played in the dance tent on Sunday and when we got off stage we found out "Hide U" had gone into the charts at number six, so we had extra reason to celebrate! Eminem turned up backstage in some small motor and jumped on stage. No production, just two decks and microphone!!! Proving you don't need a big lighting rig and loads of technicians!!!'
**Markee Substance (Kosheen – Producer)**

'I have a lot of vivid memories, the best was the year I actually played. I think it was 2001... it was so important to me to show everyone my songs but I remember getting cut off early and smashing the microphone while rockin' in my ball gown in a very teenage rock'n'roll fit. I remember meeting my future ex-boyfriend and stealing kisses in the rain backstage one year thinking no one could see our very romantic moment until it I saw it in the *NME* the following week... That's Reading for you... always a story!'
**Harry (Dirty Harry – Vocals)**

'I'd always dreamed of going over and just to be invited was amazing. I was sitting on the side of the stage watching Green Day and to my left was Chrissie Hynde and to my right was Iggy Pop... I didn't say anything, but to be in their presence and to be able hang out with Green Day as we had the same sound guy, it was just incredible.'
**Jamie Arentzen (American Hi-Fi – Vocals/Guitar)**

'We decided to make a time-capsule with the Strokes backstage. Robert Pollard stood guard as we dug a three-foot hole by the bathrooms. There was an empty tennis-bag and we each clipped off some hair and put it in the bag.
I had a sheet of song-lyrics in my pocket and I put those in there. Julian put in a bracelet, I think. Albert put in drugs and a tie. Kimya put her underwear in the bag and then we buried it pretty deep, I bet it's there still.'
**Adam Green (The Moldy Peaches – Vocals)**

'I remember us all excitedly getting dressed up, Dav and Glenn in smart shirts and eyeliner, me in a vintage black eighties dress and somehow we'd persuaded our roadies to wear tuxes and kilts. I remember peeking out from behind the stage to see how the crowd was coming along and being half humbled, half horrified that the entire tent was filling up. The gig was a bit of a blur, I felt equal parts glowing confidence, being a part of something special, and like I'd forgotten how to walk. Something set up for us by our manager was that the end of the show would be a glorious blaze of pyro-confetti cannons. The guy from the pyro company was off to one side of the stage with a trigger unit

and a wan smile, and as we struck the last chords I gave him the nod, only to see him frantically pushing the button. Dav assumed with the weight of the occasion I'd forgotten and gave an even bigger nod to both of us, before realising nothing was going to happen, and so the longest and most painful outro ended with no explosion, other than the one the pyro company got off stage for their faulty equipment. The crowd were lovely to us though, and we felt we'd done a good job.'
**Jo Taylor (Easyworld – Bass)**

'I'd been on the "Beyond Good and Evil" world tour for months and everyone knew we were coming to the UK to do Reading. I remember feeling pretty amped as we walked from the busses to the stage. I could see out into the audience from the wings, and it was just people as far as I could see. It's a huge site to take in. And then we hit the stage. The sound was fantastic, and our energy was 100%. I remember at one point walking down the runway that was under the huge PA system and turning around to notice a HUGE video screen behind me... with me on it!!' **Billy Morrison (The Cult – Bass)**

'Walking on that stage with all its history was completely exhilarating. I remember thinking, "who the fuck are we to be playing main stage at Reading when Rocket from the Crypt are playing in a tent somewhere? They're gunna throw shit at us."

'Sure enough, a couple songs into our set, let the Carling cups of beer fly. At one point, I stuck my hand up in the air and a cider bottle landed right in my hand. The crowd roared, and we laughed with them. I threw it back out to the crowd. Again, cheers. A few more songs into the set we played "Heaven is Half Pipe". Shit kept flying, but the vibe changed throughout the crowd. Kids of all styles, the Marilyn Manson kids with black hair, black fingernail polish and white-painted faces, some white-haired Eminem wannabees, punk rockers, metal heads, Brit poppers and hippies all started to sing together, with us. A song they all knew from the radio and a video they had been watching on MTV all summer. A song we wrote at my sister's house in Santa Cruz in her spare bedroom while smoking weed and

listening to all these very bands for our own inspiration. And now to be on the same bill with Iggy Pop, PJ Harvey, Rancid, the Cult and Green Day, as a fan, there are no words. That's the beauty of Reading, we all think we're so different from one another and we try to sub-categorize everything we do. But music is music, and it's one of the greatest things to bring us all together.'
**John e. (OPM – Vocals)**

'The thing that most impressed me was seeing the front man of Fun Lovin' Criminals spending most of his afternoon time on the hardcore stage and really enjoying himself while watching incredibly heavy acts. I mean, compared to what he's usually used to playing it was weird to see... it reminded me that you can't forget your roots.'
**Paolo 'Chinaski' Pavanello (Linea 77 – Guitar)**

'On both occasions that I've seen Pulp headline at Reading (2001 and 2002), Jarvis has come out with the same opening gambit, asking the crowd "Where are all your books? This is the reading festival, isn't it?" They were great both years – Jarvis always appears so at home in front of a big crowd and Pulp's biggest anthems are best performed in front of a huge, appreciative audience, especially when they're rounding off a whole day and night of live music.'
**Chris Hawkins (Radio 6 DJ)**

'When I hit the stage I was literally on more than an eighth of very potent 'shrooms.... The gig was very anticipated and well received ... I think it was Dave Ling of *Metal Hammer* that said our "Anyone" show was the toast of the festivals... What a cool guy!'
**Riz Story (Anyone – Vocals/Guitar)**

'In terms of personal memories I recall how we were obsessed about who would be playing at the same time as us. We were on at about 6.45 in the Radio One tent after Mark B and Blade and followed by one of our all time heroes, Steve Malkmus. But we were in direct competition with Queens of the Stone Age, who were all over the radio and MTV like a rash at the time. I distinctly remember thinking "no fucker will come and see us while they are playing!" then, almost to jab a hot stick into my neurosis, their frontman Josh strode out of the catering tent in front of me like the man mountain

that he is. I felt like my days in the cubs were over and now I was camping with the venture scouts. However, it was the most amazing feeling to step out onto the stage and see thousands of faces. It was just a ridiculous feeling of euphoria and we really got stuck into the set, all imagining a sense of pure unbridled achievement in our little indie lives. Then I looked stage left and saw the mighty Malkmus there checking us out, nodding away like he was into it. The crowd seem to love it and we came off stage like euphoric drunks. It was a wonderful day.'
**Dan Symons (Lowgold – Guitar)**

**BELOW: Mexican lager wave!**

# 2002

**The debut bill-topping performance for Foo Fighters proved that Dave Grohl was no longer living in the shadow of his Nirvana past. The Leeds half of the festival was headlined by Guns N' Roses, with Reading having the Prodigy. For the second year in a row, the Sunday on the mainstage was rock day, with Offspring, Slipknot, NoFX, Incubus and Puddle Of Mudd performing.**

'The first year we headlined the Reading Festival may have been the best, most fun show in the history of our band. It was the first time my now fiancé saw that I was actually a real drummer in a real band. Roger Taylor, one of my biggest heroes in the world, was on the side of the stage. His son, Rufus, was sitting right behind my kit. Although this was a very important show for us, everything just seemed right. But more importantly than all that, we happened to play better than we had ever played before in front of a ton of people. The right time, the right chemistry, and we just nailed it for some reason. That will always be one of the most meaningful and memorable gigs I have ever played.'
**Taylor Hawkins (Foo Fighters – Drums)**

'I think a girl ran onstage naked, when we were playing "Spread Your Love" and she was completely "full on", there wasn't anything left on her! No one saw how she got on there and no one saw where she went after, it was amazing. She's like the naked ghost of Reading!'
**Robert Turner (Black Rebel Motorcycle Club – Bass/Vocals)**

'We got the chance to see and meet some of our favourite bands. I'll never forget meeting Primal Scream. I remember Mani being really friendly and invited me and Stu for a beer in the dressing room. Bobby Gillespie fell out of the toilet and passed me a case of cds.'
**Robert Harvey (The Music – Vocals/Guitar)**

'I think I was really drunk, really sunburnt and there was a girl with a Mohawk and she was on some kind of drugs, because her pupils were huge. I remember Slipknot, the VIP area, and us playing really badly. The crowd was great and I felt really good. Then we went and watched it in a little truck, because they filmed it and it was like ooohhhh!!! (Not good).'
**Aaron Barrett (Reel Big Fish – Vocals/Guitar)**

'One of the coolest things about the festival is you can hear all sorts; hip-hop, rock, folk, ska bands for god's sake!! Being accepted to play a festival of that size and magnitude and prestige in the States just isn't something that happens. Being in our band that has such an eclectic mix of tastes, there's always something there to please. Everybody has something there that they will like to watch and if not, then there's no pleasing them!! There are always a lot of really attractive people walking around backstage; we like to be surrounded by attractive people because we are not attractive people!!!!'
**Scott Klopfenstein (Reel Big Fish – Trumpet/Guitar/Piano/Vocals)**

'Finally a line-up where all the bands sound good together. It seemed like every single band on the main stage was killer (I'm sure the other stages dominated as well, but I couldn't get away from all the great entertainment on the main stage). We all put on really great shows, it was exciting to be playing for eachother and side stage was packed, the weather was nice, so everyone was wandering about backstage and handing out compliments and congrats on success and whatnot. Nobody was acting awkward, nervous or better than anyone else. It was what I had always hoped playing and being backstage at festivals would be like, rock 'n' roll summer camp!'
**Zia McCabe (The Dandy Warhols – Keyboards)**

'What I remember is an autograph session I did in a tent after we played. The concert itself was amazing, especially getting to play on the main stage at our first ever Reading Festival, but what I remember most clearly is getting to talk to all the different people during the signing session afterwards. The autograph session was meant to last for an hour, but I wasn't able to finish all the people in line, so we went around to the back of the tent, and I was allowed to keep meeting people there. I think we planned on spending another two hours back there, but more and more people kept lining up to say hello. It all sort of turned into a party within a party – a festival within a festival. It really felt as though I was part of something wonderful. That feeling is best described as TOTAL LOVE. I love that day we had in Reading.'
**Andrew W.K. (Andrew W.K. – Vocals)**

Julian Casablancas, lead
singer of the Strokes

**LEFT: Maxim Reality of the Prodigy 'stares out' the crowd**

'The guy from Dashboard Confessional came up to me and Pete, telling us how Sick Of It All MADE his teenage years and helped him through his "rough spots". I thought that's great! Now go tell the world to buy our records as well!!'
**Lou Koller (Sick Of It All – Vocals)**

'We got all the kids to do a circle pit and we ended up with about five or six pits and filled the whole tent. They looked like cogs in a machine, it was just absolutely insane. There were people singing along; you remember that for ever and get complete "goose bumps", you feel privileged to be a part of it.'
**Boob (Capdown – Bass)**

'What I loved about the year 2002 was the completely different music scene. It felt like coming back to a familiar place but everything was new. To me Reading represents the music scene in the UK that I can identify with the most. It is also one of the few festivals which reflects on the rest of Europe and influences others in terms of line-up choices and music taste.'
**Alec Empire (Alec Empire – Vocals/Guitar/ Synthesizer/Sampler)**

'Throwing my guitar in the audience because I was so pissed off from all the technical difficulties we were having and watching the guitar get passed around a sea of like 15,000 people and thinking, "Fuck this IS a great show!!"'
**John Feldmann (Goldfinger – Vocals/Guitar)**

'Noble had four bushes strapped to him. He looked like a good horror movie or a bad horror movie and he climbed the central pole as the Polyphonic Spree played. People were turning around to watch him and the Polyphonic Spree were singing to him. When he came down all the bouncers jumped on "Tree Man" and he was shouting "I'M IN A BAND!" Afterwards he was signing autographs as "Tree Man", and all the stars wanted their pictures taken with him.'
**Yan (British Sea Power – Vocals/Guitar)**

'I do remember one specific moment from the show itself. Our guitarist Cahir, during a long musical breakdown section, went so ape that his lead went flying out of his guitar. Not

**BELOW: Getting 'hot 'n' sweaty' in the pit**

normally too much of a problem but for some reason, which he has never really explained, he was unable to find the end of his own lead. I remember clearly looking over at him as he wandered aimlessly around for what seemed like ages – his hands on his hips, then scratching his head in a Charlie Chaplin-style act of bewilderment – in front of the large crowd searching in vain for his own lead.

'My brother Raife (our drummer) and I mouthed the words "keep going" to eachother as we played the same riff over and over as Cahir's search went on and on. With great delight, he found it hidden under his own monitor. His little face lit up. He plugged back in, deep breaths all round as we carried on. Despite how it sounds we played well and I was on such a high afterwards I thought my heart might explode.'
**Jamie Burchell (Jetplane Landing – Bass)**

'DJ was supposed to open the show going back and forth on the decks with Moby Dick by Led Zeppelin – but it wasn't happening and the crowd was impatient and started booing. But by the end they were freaking out and going crazy, which was cool. Peaches came by and was dancing in the front part where the cameras were.

They picked my rider as one of the funniest – I asked for socks, batteries, stickers that said "London" on them (I used to put tourist stickers over my boobs wherever I was playing and flash the audience), lollipops, and two pairs of thong underwear. But I didn't really know why my rider was so funny...?'
**Princess Superstar (DJ/Singer)**

'I was working at the festival, doing backstage interviews for BBC6 Music. I remember Courtney Taylor, lead singer with the Dandy Warhols, saying he'd spare just two minutes to talk. I was keen to get an interview out of him, so I agreed that two minutes would suffice. We sat down just outside their changing room and the response to my first question was nine minutes long! The interview ended up running for 48 minutes, as Courtney enthused about Reading Festival and playing in the UK.'
**Chris Hawkins (Radio 6 DJ)**

'Within ten minutes of parking me and a few of the band and a couple of our crew went for a walk around the artists' enclosure to see what we could get for breakfast, as we'd been playing a gig the night before and were all hung over. After breakfast we went back to the bus, got some clean clothes and went for a shit, shave and shower (minus the endless queues and minging toilets). As soon as that chore was done, the free beer tent was our destination, where we happily stayed for a few hours watching all the industry cocksuckers namedropping about bands they knew. Late afternoon after a mad panic our tour manager finally found us and all hell broke out as we were due on in half an hour and were still completely pissed. The atmosphere on the concrete jungle stage was mind blowing as we were faced with a blur of faces, with kids hanging off poles and ropes left, right and centre as they tried to wedge into the stupidly overcrowded marquee. The performance for us was exceptionally good as adrenaline (and beer) took over and the shouts and crowd-surfing finished off a brilliant show, although security probably wouldn't agree after being made to work for once.'
**Damon 'Des' Robins (Spunge – Guitar)**

'I remember getting the sofa out of our portakabin and watching everyone walking past.'
**Jem King (Spunge – Drums)**

'The after show was like most fests: drinking, drugs and a lot off bullshit – but that's the music biz for ya. Didn't get to meet any famous people that I can remember but I'm sure I made a pratt of myself at some point of the evening. Since our chance to play both Reading and Leeds I've never been back, how cool? The only time I went was to play a gig, not many people can say that.'
**Wol Gurney (Spunge – Guitar)**

'Highlight was definitely the Foos, who headlined on Saturday with a spectacular firework display as an encore. There was a guy dressed as Spiderman. He was mentioned by a lot of the bands and appeared on the big screen a number of times. As far as we could work out, he didn't take the mask off all weekend.

'Watched the White Stripes on the Saturday afternoon, sat on the grassy verge eating melon, very chilled. Had the obligatory bonfire on the Sunday night, burn everything you own including your tent, sleeping bag, clothes and car keys. Managed to nick someone's gazebo and stow it home. It now lives in my mums shed as contraband!'
**Darcus Shannon (Festival – Part-timer)**

Show us your horns!

# 2003

White Stripes cancelled after Jack White's car crash, to be replaced by a nervous Black Rebel Motorcycle Club, who managed to pull it off. Jay Z cancelled on the Friday, which gave the chance for emerging stars The Darkness to 'leap frog' up the bill, much to the pleasure of the crowd. The Libertines made their debut on the main stage without Pete Doherty, who was having problems with the band. Sunday was rock day, with the 'Mighty Metallica', System of a Down, Sum 41, All American Rejects and Biffy Clyro. Early on Sunday afternoon Good Charlotte were bottled and pelted for their whole set.

'We weren't even planning to play Reading, and then White Stripes cancelled when Jack White broke his finger. For a couple of weeks I guess they didn't know what they were going to do and they asked us a few days before; I think we said no. Then we talked about it and decided we would cover one of their songs "The Hardest Button to Button" (that was my favourite song on that record). So we figured we'd do that, dedicate it and try and get in their good graces. Before I went on I saw Meg there, who I guess was doing press, and to apologise for what had happened I told her that we were going to cover this song, and she was like "that's cool and no big deal." People got into it and it was actually one of the best shows that we've ever done. It was shocking!'

**Robert Turner (Black Rebel Motorcycle Club – Bass/Vocals)**

'I was walking around backstage desperate for a pee. I found a disgusting gents toilet. I thought: No, don't fancy this much. So I dived into the empty Ladies one. Then a guy in a hat (maybe with a feather in it?) came out of one of the traps. He washed up. So did I. Then we walked out and he turned to me and said, "Hey kid, bit of advice for you – when you're at a festival, always use the Ladies, they're clean as fuck." It was Ian Brown.'

**Colin MacIntyre (Mull Historical Society – Vocals/Guitar)**

'Honestly, it was like a dream come true, it was like "there we are, out there!!". We had spoofed Staind and Limp Bizkit in one of our videos and Staind were parked next to us and Limp Bizkit were playing right after us!! It was a really cool day, a really, really cool day!! Just amazing! I have this picture on my TV at home, where I say "everybody flip Erik off" and everybody gives Erik the finger. There's about 60,000 people saying "fuck you Erik!!"'

**Jaret Reddick (Bowling For Soup – Vocals/Guitar)**

'I got to bring my then girlfriend (who is now my wife) and my sister with me, and that was an amazing thing to have

them there on the side of the stage as we played to the largest audience that we had ever played for at that point. My sister took a photo from the side of the stage that day that made it onto our tour poster that we sell at our merchandise booth every night at shows. Jaret, for some reason, said to everybody to "flip Erik off", so everybody gave me the finger. The photo that made it onto our poster is my silhouette, from the back, with 86,000 people giving me the finger.'

**Erik Chandler (Bowling For Soup – Bass)**

'It was drizzling with rain that might as well have been LSD from the audience's perspective. The stage was half-wired up and the crowd was ecstatic almost to a fault; the entire spectacle indeed seemed like some insane hippie gathering from the summer of '67. The set cascaded with an energy that was full of perpetual motion that was fuelled on the fear of not being able to ever stop the machine that had been started. Wet from the rain, the sweat of the stage and crowd, we left with a sense of disbelief that this thing had ever happened.'

**The Polyphonic Spree**

'It was the first show that we ever played in England and probably the most painful. Hangovers, induced by the *Kerrang!* Awards after party the night before and compounded by an unfamiliar jet lag, really knocked the crap out of us before our 2pm set time. Every word that I spat out of my mouth gave me a crushing pain in the head; it was as if my head was being squeezed in a vice. The crowd seemed thrilled; but I know we were not at our best, several of us puking after our set would probably confirm that suspicion. We couldn't last the rest of the day and loaded the van to head for some needed rest after our set. However, our "one word review" in the NME read "Satanic!" Pretty good, I guess?'

**Jon Gallant (Billy Talent – Bass/Vocals)**

'The fact is that one of my rituals before I go on stage is pissing in a bottle. So there I was, Linkin Park's massive crew on one side of me setting all their gear, 80,000 plus people on

The 'Mighty' Metallica headline 'Metal Sunday'

the other side of me, and a glut of stage crew running around me in a whirlwind and all I could think about was that I have to piss in bottle. I ducked behind some Linkin Park cases to commence with my ritual, but was quickly brushed away as they needed to polish cymbals or fix a computer or some such nonsense. "AH HA!"

'Right behind the stack of guitar amps, what a perfect spot, shielded from a constant flow of techs and press, score! I had three minutes till we played the biggest show of our band's history and I'm pissing in a bottle behind a stack of guitar cabinets, it was comedy. As I was pissing I couldn't help but reading LP's set list taped up against a scuffed guitar box, around the fourth song it had a note that said "...thank Metallica.". Reading Festival, thank you for having us grace the stage and also thank you for booking headliners with massive guitar stacks for me to piss behind."
**Vinnie Fiorello (Less Than Jake – Drums)**

'I remember when we played and Metallica was headlining. We'd all been huge fans of Metallica since we were kids, but I don't think any of us had seen them live before and then there we were, on the side stage, watching them perform to 100,000 people. It was the most thrilling performance I'd ever witnessed and I thanked God we didn't have to go on afterwards.'
**Steve Jocz (Sum 41 – Drums)**

"There was "Piss Pants". It was the first time that we had taken mushrooms before the show and we got down to blue undies covered in beer, which looked like 'Piss Pants'."
**Hamilton (British Sea Power – Bass/Vocals/Guitar)**

'I'll always remember turning up round the back and seeing clouds of dust floating in the air and thinking it's like Armageddon in here. The kids are up for it and they ain't leaving without their money's worth and that's how a festival should be.'
**Simon Franks (Audio Bully's – Sampler/Piano/ Drums/Vocals)**

'I have to admit, I knew very little about the festival's history prior to us performing. The fact that the Reading Festival is so diverse made my experience there more exciting. I was really blown away with how many different stages there were at the festival and how many people dedicated themselves to staying around all day and night. The one lasting memory of Reading was the crowd's energy from the time we started to the time we left. The show was crazy and I can't say that I have had the same experience playing anywhere else in the world. For some reason or another, that night at Reading was pure magic for me.'
**John Collura (The Ataris – Guitar/Pianos)**

'I was sat backstage in my tent and a man came around selling weed and I thought "yeah, this is a good idea". So, I bought an eighth of weed off him and he got it out of the wrap and showed it to me and as he did he dropped it on the grass in front of my tent and he picked most of it up and put it back in the packet. For the rest of the weekend I smoked about a yard square of the grass in front of my tent, just to make sure that I got it all!!!'
**John Harper (The Cooper Temple Clause – Drums/ Gretsch Drums/DW Snares/Sabian Cymbals/Percussion/ Backing Vocals)**

'We use old vintage gear, a 100 watt vocal PA, drum kit with all the skins on, no sound man, so their chaps had to just dangle some mics over us to try to capture our sound. We aren't a rock group and don't like large gigs, but the sound men were old school and knew exactly what we were up to, so it was a great sound, close to our normal back room noise. They thought we were the best thing since sliced toast, all the corporate junk being played at you, from hidden discos in every corner. I don't like crowds or outdoor music much.'
**Billy Childish (Buff Medways – Vocals/Guitar)**

'All our friends were playing with us, but I was excited about playing with the Buff Medways and Billy Bragg. Both Billy's had been idols of mine.  Billy Childish has one of the best senses of humor in the business. That has always shined through in his records like a beacon of light. And he is tops on guitar and recording technique. So imagine how excited I was to turn around, after loading a 100lb amplifier into the van, to find him extending his hand for a shake. I was very disappointed in our showing at the festival, but he wasn't. Surprisingly, he was a bit shy, I think. He kept looking at the ground when I was talking to him. He was trying to stick a two foot piece of toilet paper to his shoe. I saw this and suggested that he spit on the toilet paper and it will follow him around all day. He took the advice and ran with it.  When the Buff Medways took the stage he marched out with said paper in tow. Military salute and shirt pulled thru the fly of his trousers were added for effect. Peter Sellers lives. Billy Bragg on the other hand didn't catch our set. But he did catch a glimpse of my red and grey stripped pants. He mentioned that if we mixed his tasselled cowboy shirt with my pants we would be dangerous. Mr Bragg is the epitome of the selfless musician. This was my

third time meeting him in the past 15 years and he always makes you feel as if you are an old mate.'
**Johnnie Walker (Soledad Brothers – Vocals/Guitar)**

'I remember a guy in a German army helmet in the moshpit, I don't know what he was doing there, but he was pretty terrifying! We had a small van, we turned up and Metallica and Foo Fighters were there, they'd cordoned off the toilets, it was a bit of a circus. Metallica had a little room backstage where they were practising and our friend tried to take a photo, but these people pounced on him and took the camera, he never saw that again. We were thrown out of Reading for arguing with Good Charlotte,'
**Ben Perrier (Winnebago Deal – Guitar/Vocals)**

'When showtime came, we managed to pummel our way through a rollicking set on someone else's equipment (the gear rental guy had mixed up our order), and we ended with the dance. There were about 5000 people crammed into the tent, and when the routine ended, I swear every single one of them was screaming. I could see flailing arms bouncing off the rubber rear wall. I should be embarrassed to say it, but that dance may have been our most triumphant moment ever.'
**Damian Kulash (OK Go – Vocals/Guitar)**

'I was wandering around drinking when I ran into Bobby Gillespie. I broke down and asked if could get my picture taken with him; he was friendly and said in his thick Scots accent, "sure, as long as you quit drinking that crap beer and get a proper one from our dressing room!" I snapped the shot, which he made me do over, 'cos he didn't like the way his face looked. We headed to their dressing room where I met Mani, Throb, and Kevin Shields (formerly of another fav Brit band, My Bloody Valentine). They handed me a Swedish lager and we did a few shots of whiskey. Kevin was rolling a joint. We all hung out and talked about music for a while. Getting loaded with the Primal Scream further fuelled my romantic ideal of what a huge British festival like Reading was all about!'
**Marko 72 (Sugarcult – Guitar)**

'Most wonderful moments that are highly anticipated usually seem so fleeting upon revisiting. Our performance early that evening seemed to last no more than thirty seconds. I couldn't help but feel overwhelmed by the magnificence of the crowd, and the sentiment that I had never felt more alive as a musician. I managed to store as much of what took place that weekend where nobody will ever be able to take it from me.

I am grateful that I knew then that moments as significant as Reading and Leeds usually only come along only once for most musicians. A month or so after our only appearance, we split ways as a band. Even though I revisit that weekend often in the viaducts of my own mind, I have not been back across the Ocean since.'
**Dan Navetta (The Movielife – Guitar)**

'Bizarrely enough, the Orange tent backstage were throwing all day beach parties and had requested our DJing skills on the Saturday afternoon, which meant we "treated" the clientele with a selection of black metal, obscure hardcore and the occasional blast of 80's go go funk.'
**Joe Birch (Hell is For Heroes – Drums)**

'It was the first time that we were playing live in the UK and a lot of people turned up to see us. One thing that really impressed me was how all the bands hung out together in backstage and catering and so I got to meet a whole bunch of people that I had always wanted to meet. But the one person that I didn't get to meet was Beck, as I am a huge fan, but I got to meet his band. It was all very social.'
**Amanda Tannen (Stellastarr* – Bass)**

'Part of the fun of those festivals for us is to go around the big stages and VIP areas (we usually play in the smaller "Concrete Jungle") and see what kind of famous people we can spot. One year we decided to turn the tables... our trombone player Eddie is Mexican but he looks a lot like Sascha Baron Cohen (only much shorter...). We happened to have a camouflage jumpsuit on the bus, a little hat and some eyeliner for his moustache and, lo and behold, Ali G was backstage!'
**Brian Flenniken (Mad Caddies – Drums)**

**Radio One's Jo Whiley**

# 2004

The Darkness proved how massive they were in 2004, by topping the bill, after only making their debut at the festival the year before; but this was to be their Reading swan song. The New York Dolls gave a classic performance on Saturday afternoon, with Sami Yaffa (ex- Hanoi Rocks) on bass, making his return to the festival after 21 years. Lostprophets nearly killed the crowd with their 'Wall of Death' stunt; Kaiser Chiefs made their debut on the Carling stage and ticket prices went over £100.00 for the first time, costing £105.00.

'When you go to the Leeds Festival, the Reading part of it is always seen as the more important part by the journalists and people "down south" and there is a certain amount of resentment from people from the north, about that whole hierarchy of it!!!! But we went down and it was brilliant, it was a lot of fun! It was my first real taste of being in a band, because we had just started, literally just started! When we started, we just thought we'd start a band and hopefully get on at the Leeds Festival, just to get free tickets and get in and hang around backstage and spot the pop stars. But, we also got to play the Reading Festival.

'We travelled down and my feeling was I'd been to festivals all my life and I'd been blagging my way in using different tricks, but the weird thing was I was backstage expecting someone to throw me out any minute, because there was that feeling that I shouldn't really be here, but then it dawned on me that I was allowed and it was the first time I had a legitimate reason. I was wandering around backstage, and I was in a band and I was looking at all these people dressed totally inappropriately for the festival, and it was then that I realised that backstage at festivals the people who look most like pop stars are least likely to be pop stars, and the real pop stars are the ones prepared with the wellies and cagoules. The others were all in their stilettos and bikini tops and flared trousers that have soaked up so much mud.

'The experience was great and I quite liked the closeness of it all, it felt like being in just a huge club. We were in the small bands' tent and we were about third on, basically we were the lowest of the low and no one gave a shit! But it was full and we felt like stars! Because only pop stars are allowed to play the Reading Festival and we were allowed to play it!

'Morrissey played as well and I'd never seen him before, I'd got all his records and my jaw was on the floor. I learnt a lot by watching him and it was then that I had another epiphany about entertainment. A band's job is entertainment, that's what they're for. A lot of bands over the last few years think their job is being rock stars and being cool. But that's not the job at all, the job is entertainment and the job is making people have a better day by seeing you and connecting, exactly what Morrissey does. I think, hopefully, the Kaiser Chiefs do that.'
**Ricky Wilson (Kaiser Chiefs – Vocals/Tambourine)**

'Going up to Reading I was a bit worried really, because of the London crowd, as opposed to our hometown crowd. I was a bit nervous and didn't know what to expect, but I seem to remember it went really well. I remember watching Franz early on in the afternoon and thinking that we needed to try and catch them and we then heard how much they were being paid and it was like "WOW! that's amazing!!" To see Franz play it spurred us on a little bit, because people were touting us as the next Franz Ferdinand. So we tried to achieve that and more.'
**Nick 'Peanut' Baines (Kaiser Chiefs – Keyboard)**

'I went to the Reading Festival from '92 to '98, camping and camping it up! Saw everyone including Kula Shaker. It was the only true rock festival. I didn't want to go to Glastonbury, because it was just full of hippies. I preferred it when it was just the Reading Festival and they always got the big headliners, like the Stone Roses.'
**Andrew 'Whitey' White (Kaiser Chiefs – Guitar)**

'I had to find a parking space on the street, as opposed to being actually allowed into the complex, as we were fairly unrecognisable. We were just happy that anyone came to see us really.'
**Nick Hodgson (Kaiser Chiefs – Drums/Vocals)**

'We were wondering how we were going to go down. We'd toured around America and the UK, but we hadn't done a show in the UK for a while. We walked on and kicked into the first song and it all went off, it was incredible. It's hard to put into words, but the vibe was that everyone was into it. It was like everyone was happy for us and everyone was backing us. It was very humbling and it felt like everyone was really proud that we were from the UK.

Morrissey on stage

The Hives invite the crowd onstage

'It just kept building up and building up to the point we played "Last Train Home" and I did a little speech and when we kicked into it the whole place was jumping up and down at the same time. I do watch it on "You Tube" whenever I'm feeling depressed! Right towards the end of the set, I had this stupid idea. Because we'd been doing this thing called "The Wall Of Death", where we split the crowd in two, Braveheart style, and then when the song kicks in they run at each other. But the thing was we'd be playing shows with 2000 people and it was a laugh, but looking back I don't know what the fuck I was thinking. Seriously, it could have gone so wrong and we haven't done it since, if you're not going to better it, there's no point. So, basically, we split the crowd, right down the middle and, because we have a song called "Shinobivsdragonninja" I called one side Shinobi and the other Dragon Ninja. I was firing them up, saying "Are you ready, are you ready?" and I explained that when the song kicked in they run at each other. As far as the eye could see the crowd was split, with a clear gap right down the middle, where people could run up and down. The song kicked in and everyone just ran at each other! But weird thing was, they ran at each other and compacted in the middle, but the outside people didn't stop running and they were piling up on each other. I remember looking round and everybody's faces were like "WHAT ARE YOU DOING?" Our tour manager had his head in his hands, going "This is it, we're going to jail!"

'But to this day, people still come up to us and say "Reading 2004 man, that Wall of Death, fuckin' amazing!!"'
**Ian Watkins (Lostprophets – Vocals)**

'The best part for me was going out in the crowd at night, taking in the all the sounds, sights and smells. The fires and faces in the dark create such a dramatic and beautiful scene. Strolling through the field feeling all the millions of moments and seeing thousands of beautiful faces flashing in and out of the smoky dim was the most memorable part of the festival.'
**Greg Attonito (Bouncing Souls – Vocals)**

'The Dolls at Reading was a complete opposite in a way. The same mud etc.... but the kids were very nice and well behaved, not like the rabid dogs of '83. We hit the stage and the sun came out. Played a great set of the legendary brilliant New York Dolls' songs that I'm honoured to play. It was like a very nice camping-trip, compared to the '83 madness. Times they do change....'
**Sami Yaffa (New York Dolls – Bass)**

'It's crazy trying to get around there to see all the bands. I remember that the last time we were there, I stayed on stage for the whole J5 (Jurassic 5) concert and I was pretty obsessed with that. I like the mix of musical genres that was at the field. I ran out on the stage and tripped and fell and tackled my trombone off the stand and stood up like it was a gymnastic feat.'
**Dan Regan (Reel Big Fish – Trombone)**

'We had waited to play the Reading Festival for ten years. Year after year, Wildhearts' t-shirts would feature prominently in the audience of the festival, prompting the fans, year after year, to put in a petition, signed by thousands, to get us on the bill. And every year the petition would be ignored. Then one year we got asked to support The Darkness on their European and US tours, and suddenly the organisers wanted us on the bill.'
**Ginger (The Wildhearts – Vocals/Guitar)**

'Fast forward to the end of the day, and I was walking to our dressing room, minding my own business, and this big muthafucker grabs me and throws me against the wall. I was like "get your fucking hands off me" and I took out my laminate and I was like "what the hell is going on?" He said "just stay there man". Then this cavalcade of Mercedes mini vans came in with tinted windows and I was like "is Tony Blair here?" and he said "no man it's Fiddy" and I was like "Fiddy who?" and he said "Fiddy Cent". I said "are you fucking kidding me, you just put your hands on me because some rap guy thinks I'm gonna shoot him?"

'So he takes the stage and a bottle of piss hits him in the chest and sprays him in the chest, it was one of the shortest sets, but I heard he still got paid though! But to their credit, the people who come out and rule that festival on those days, those are the people that decide who sinks and who swims. It's all well and good at the practice base, but the people aren't dumb and that's what I like about the festival.'
**Al Barr (The Dropkick Murphys – Vocals)**

'As Angela (my wife and manager, Angela Davis) and I were roaming the perimeter of the fenced main stage area, a huge pool of mud and paper cups ringed with vendors and concessions, we managed with total difficulty to get inside, and locate our merchandise tent at the utmost rear of the grounds. What we saw at the opposite end of all of this was the MAIN STAGE. A huge platform, with side-banked video screens that projected the images of the performers, who happened to be Jack and Meg White, aka The White Stripes. While Meg was totally invisible from where I was standing,

Tim Wheeler of
Ash sets fire to his
'Flying V'

Dropkick Murphys' stage invasion

Jack was, well, about the size of one digit of my finger... about one inch tall. The image on the screen, however, was larger than life, but jumped about in ever-changing camera angles. The sound was boomy, and shrill. All at once it stopped. I said to Angela, "They're done... that was the last song". I was wondering could that be it? Fifty, 60, or 70,000 people, and it's over; no encore? What kind of shit is this? What are all those people thinking? Just at that moment, the humongous video screens showed a couple somewhere in the crowd. A guy was carrying a girl on his shoulders. Almost on cue, she pulled up her t-shirt, revealing two well-appointed breasts and a gleeful smile. Fifty to 60 or 70,000 people, almost on cue, responded with gleeful appreciation. I smelled an encore. Sure enough, the titties-on-giant screen extravaganza began. Almost on cue Jack White appeared on the stage, one inch in height, guitar in hand, and proceeded to plow through another number, oblivious to what had happened on the giantrons. Ha ha ha ha. He thought the crowds were cheering for more of the White Stripes. Well that was the first time I ever saw tits get an encore. But what are you gonna do? Better take it any way you can get it! That's what I say.'
**Michael Davis (DKT/MC5 – Bass)**

'By the time the DKT/MC5 band went onstage we had had three months of continuous time together, having just toured the USA, Australia and Japan. We had our stage legs. We had heat. The band played strong and tight. Great crowd. Great response. I was overjoyed at the warm welcome we received by the audience. At first, I really didn't know how they would respond, but by the time we were halfway through the set, it was pure comfort zone and straight-ahead rock 'n' roll. I personally wish to thank everyone in attendance.'
**Dennis Thompson (DKT/MC5 – Drums)**

'Music, rock 'n' roll, is a thing that is supposed to unite people from different backgrounds, continents, races. When I played Reading 2004... some people in the audience were very violent, throwing stuff on stage and so on... showing a lot of anger. For many people in Britain success of The Rasmus came fast, maybe too fast. Even Bob Dylan was booed at Newport Folk Music Festival in 1965, when he played electric Chicago blues in the heyday of the genre. For some people it appeared as a fake copy by a whitey... and what is his status today? Well, anyway, we'll come after a year or two and make it all up for the fans who didn't get the show that they paid for.'
**Eero (The Rasmus – Bass)**

'The MC5 still rock like motherfuckers, 50 Cent's Gangster buffoonery got him hounded of the stage and the most violent and aggressive bouncers we have ever wound up nearly stomped us before we had even found the free bar. Our gig was a lot of fun. It feels like you have a responsibility to start the day with some excitement when you're on at 12 noon. God bless the few hundred who were watching at such a weird time of day for a gig and god bless our tour manager who got us there on time (and saved us from the bouncers).'
**George Riley (10,000 Things – Bass/Backing Vocals)**

'Goldfinger was being chanted so loud I couldn't hear myself or the band. Seeing 20,000 people jumping at the same time during "Counting The Days" was totally surreal. All the dreams I had as a kid of being in a band were fulfilled at that moment. It was the most amazing show ever.... Having played Reading has been and honour and a privilege. The fans in England respect music more than in America. They are so dedicated to the festival events. They'll handcuff themselves to a case of beer because they know they are going to pass out and don't want anyone to steal their beer. The English really know how to do a festival....'
**John Feldmann (Goldfinger – Vocals/Guitar)**

'Yeah, mud. From the first minute of the day till we bailed out of there, it was mud. Fucking mud, no rain, just mud. Good bands... great bands on our stage, Pretty Girls Make Graves, McClusky, and mud.
**Danko Jones (Danko Jones – Vocals/Guitar)**

'When the show began, I remember feeling like walking onto this stage in front of thousands of kids was truly not a reality. For a band that mostly plays DIY venues and basements in the States, this crowd was nothing like we had experienced. When I came up to the mic and said "Hello ladies and gentlemen, we are Read Yellow" the applause of the crowd nearly knocked me on my back. Immediately, the kids in the crowd made us feel so welcome and so comfortable, that we proceeded to play one of the most enjoyable sets we have ever performed. I loved the kids, it made me want to just come off the stage and hug every one of them.

'To meet your heroes is also a very rare thing for any person to experience. I was surrounded by musicians that I respected so highly because they had created art that inspired me to also try and create. Watching Morrisey and The Libertines from the side of the stage, meeting Franz Ferdinand, seeing thousands

of people have a great time, these are the things that I was experiencing with my best friends and I couldn't have been happier.'
**Evan Kenney (Read Yellow – Vocals/Guitar)**

'To understand this experience, one must understand the backstage. Behind each stage there are these trailer type things that the bands use for their backstage quarters. Every band gets one and then has to vacate it a few hours after they play. Each backstage trailer is roughly 50 to 100 feet behind the stage. We were going to go check out Morrissey, and we see this limousine parked next to one of the trailers. We both kind of laughed a little bit and wondered what the hell a limo was doing back in all this mud and grass. Low and behold, Morrissey pops out of his trailer, hops in the limo, and gets driven 50 feet to the stage. We couldn't believe it. The dude is so rock that walking 50 is out of the question. Dude needs a limo. Amazing. Needless to say I felt feeble and poor as we loaded up the splitter van. Great times.'
**Joby Ford (The Bronx – Guitar/Vocals)**

'My initial memory is arriving at the festival and following the roads littered with revellers and beer crates in to the grounds, with everyone looking into the van to see which "important" band was arriving. It's a strange feeling, like being caught between a party and a war zone. My memory is pretty foggy, trying to remember details of the gig and backstage goings-on, only that everyone was trying to stay out of the way of Mark Lanegan, who'd just been told he had to cut his set by five songs (he's a big guy).'
**Toby Butler (The Duke Spirit – Bass)**

'Kurt Cobain's smashed up guitar from Nirvana's legendary 1991 performance was among the remarkable relics of "Music, Mud and Mayhem", celebrating 30 years of the Reading Festival. The exhibition, staged at the Museum of Reading in 2004, brought to life the story of the music festival and its importance to Reading. The exhibition launch party was buzzing, with the *Reading Evening Post* commenting that "stars turned out in force." Radio One DJ Steve Lamacq opened the show, along with Mean Fiddler boss Melvin Benn, who was reconciled with Harold Pendleton (who originally established the Festival in Reading), as they came face-to-face for the first time in over ten years. Star exhibits, in addition to Cobain's guitar (on loan from the Hard Rock Cafe in Boston, USA), included items from the Police, the Stranglers, Genesis and a pristine signed Foo Fighters guitar. Also on display

was the set list from Thin Lizzy's final UK gig in 1983, a Black Sabbath sweatband and signed memorabilia from local boys the Cooper Temple Clause. And on the walls, amongst the photographs and vintage posters, there was space for visitors to add their own favourite festival moment. You can read some of those memories and search the A-Z of bands that have played the main stage and view archive photographs online at www.readingmuseum.org.uk/festival
**Cat John (Communications Officer Reading Museum)**

'We loved the festival and the free food rider was enough for a week. We met lots of drunk, backstabbing industry freeloaders in the guest area; isn't that what the guest area is for? They don't even go to watch the bands, unless they're the embryonic Libertines-a-like sensation for that week. But the actual MUSIC festival was fucking cool!'
**Raph Brous (Riff Random – Guitar/Vocals)**

'I think the thing about Reading is it is probably the most unpretentious festival there is. The kids go there because there are bands on the list they want to see. The people that organise it know that and so they do book bands that people want to see and stay one step ahead of the "trends", or they bypass the trends completely.'
**Preston (The Ordinary Boys – Vocals/Guitar**

'Usually, in Tokyo, we play in a venue that holds about 200 people and have not played many open air shows. So, it was really an interesting experience. The stage felt really good, released! Backstage, I was excited to meet my favourite bands, plus had fun playing pinball.'
**Yoshiko 'Ronnie' Fujiyama (The 5, 6, 7, 8's – Vocals/Guitar)**

'Flying mud, flying shit, flying booze, flying tampons... the stuff of legends that makes Reading soar above other festivals. Well maybe soar is the wrong word, but as a kid growing up in Ireland that's what you heard about... the carnage, Dante's inferno, rock 'n' roll suicide. All the things you don't want to know before your first time playing there.... The gig itself was a haze of nerves and energy. A 45-minute set lasted 15, for all we remember. But one thing is certain... the crowd were amazing.'
**Dave King (Flogging Molly – Vocals/Guitar/Banjo/ Bodhran/Spoons)**
**& Bridget Regan (Flogging Molly – Fiddle/Tin Whistle/ Uilleann Pipes)**

# 2005

**Friday night heralded the triumphant return of the Pixies as headliners. Equally triumphant was the return of the Foo Fighters on Saturday and Iron Maiden on Sunday, 23 years since their last performance. The order of the weekend was guitar based pop on Saturday, with Bloc Party, Maximo Park, Editors, the Futureheads and the Rakes all appearing. Sunday, again, was full to the brim with rock, featuring Iggy and the Stooges, Incubus, Marilyn Manson, NoFX and Bullet For My Valentine. My Chemical Romance made their debut on Friday at the festival, playing Leeds main stage in the morning and Reading in the afternoon, due to award show commitments in the USA.**

'I like all the English festivals and this is a very famous one. Everyone was like "Have you played Reading yet???" So, now we've played Reading and it feels great, like all the other great festivals in England. I love it."
**David Keuning (The Killers – Guitar)**

'It was going to be the biggest audience we'd played to at that time and we didn't know what to expect, as we'd never done a festival. We were at the end of a tour where we'd been playing to 300 people in venues and these were the finishing two dates of the tour. We've got footage of us backstage and the tour manager says "are you ready then?" and you can hear them all chanting "MONKEYS", proper shouting it! All day we'd watched other bands from the side of the stage and there were people at the front who'd got there early with our t-shirts on! That was dedication for a start, and then they were chanting – and we walked on. The cameraman walked on with us and it was the loudest thing I've ever heard. The first two songs we were nervous, it was really strange. But it was still exciting.'
**Matt Helders (Arctic Monkeys – Drums)**

Dave Grohl returns to Reading

'I got absolutely hammered after we played, because it was so easy. We went to the backstage area and hung out with some of our new friends that we had made through months of touring; it was nice to catch up with bands like the Nine Black Alps and The Cribs, the kind of bands that were on the same "new cycle" as us. The problem for punters is that there's not anywhere very nearby that you can get booze from, apart from Waitrose and that's far too expensive. There's all these grubby rockers with mud all over them and dripping with sweat and they walk into Waitrose and they are suddenly with the middle classes of Reading, and it's not the easiest of combinations!!'
**Ed Lay (Editors – Drums)**

Iron Maiden claim victory on 'Metal Sunday'

'I think we knew we had arrived when we got to play Reading. Besides hearing about how big it was, how fun, all the bands that went before etc. I wore a special gold Viking superhero kind of outfit just for the occasion. Got to watch the Kills from the side of the stage. The sun was shining and, most cosmically, Reading goes down as something hugely significant for the Licks because that's where we met Dave Grohl, who ended up drumming on our next record "Four On The Floor"!

'We made a lot of Licks Lovers that day and met/saw a lot of exciting bands that will surely be around for many more Reading Festivals to come. Arcade Fire, the Kooks, the Kills, and Arctic Monkeys, just to name a few. Long live rock 'n' roll, and keep on fighting the good fight!'
**Juliette Lewis (Juliette and the Licks – Vocals)**

'Reading is probably the festival that's closest to my heart, because I've been coming for years and years, ever since I left college. Friday night it was always the place to be. I've seen so many great bands and had so many great moments there. Apart from coming as a punter and seeing bands like New Order there, I have also done my show from there many times and had some amazing moments, with the Yeah,Yeah,Yeahs, The Datsuns, Incubus, Travis and The Darkness. We've had some really great times. It's a really special festival for me.'
**Jo Whiley (Radio 1 DJ)**

'Reading will be memorable not only for the brilliant crowd, but for the loss of all the clothing I was wearing on my upper body. I became extremely forgetful, in part due to my appearance on stage with The Rakes earlier on in the day. I was nervous for a change, since it wasn't our crowd and I didn't know the words to the songs that well. I gave it all I had and was rewarded by a member of Towers of London jumping on my back at the end of the two songs I performed. Backstage, I caught a glimpse of the beautiful Dita Von Teese, which made my day.'
**Paul Smith (Maximo Park – Vocals)**

'Walking out as the first band on the Sunday morning slot was always going to be a weird one, taking into account their hangovers and ours. But when I looked down and eyeballed the Bloc Party white gaffer-tape all over the floor, then looked up and saw a couple of thousand friendly faces, I knew we had reached a huge milestone and the fun took off from there. Kicking off with "Back Again" I immediately felt the rush that so many have felt over the years on that stage. I don't know if it's true, but a couple of minutes before going on someone said that we were the first unsigned band to play on the Radio

One stage in years, so that added to the buzz, but as we were playing through the set I felt like we deserved to be there.'
**Chris Peck (Boy Kill Boy – Vocals/Guitar)**

'The circumstances under which we played were unusual, because Alan our singer was unwell. We'd been touring in Japan, he was run down and needed some time off. Basically, his throat was gone and he couldn't sing! We were originally going to pull out, but thought we'd give it a go, with me doing vocals, because I do a bit of backing vocals on the record anyway. It was very nerve-wracking for all of us, going up there without our focal point, because in any band the singer IS the focal point. It was a big tent and a lot of people in there, so I went onstage and said that our singer was unable to be there, and the entire crowd went "OOOOOHHHHH!" But once we got into our stride, it was really good. The good thing was we had a trump card up our sleeve!! We had asked Bloc Party (who we'd toured with that year), Maximo Park (who we'd played with a lot) and Towers of London (who we share management with) and they all came on. Paul from Maximo Park sang "Strasbourg" and "22 Grand Job" and he did it really well, in his Northern accent. We were rehearsing it backstage and, because he didn't know all the words, he wrote them down in a book and he used the book as a prop and it looked really interesting. Gordon and Russell from Bloc Party came on and there was quite a melee of people at the end!'
**Matthew Swinnerton (The Rakes – Guitar)**

'Playing on the Radio One stage was a massive deal for us and me personally. For the previous five years I had attended Reading as a punter, each time thinking "one day we'll be on one of those stages." When that day came it was unreal and unforgettable. Having now been to hundreds of festivals, I must admit my opinion of Reading is different. It's no longer top of the heap. It's top of the pops!'
**Ian Catskilkin (Art Brut – Guitar)**

'The line up was quite eclectic and I was surprised that there were so many people in the tent and up for the dance experience at an essentially rock festival. Our set was quite short and unfortunately without one of our singers, but the response from the mainly young crowd was awesome and kind of took us by surprise.... The energy and live aspects of our band seem to have struck a chord with younger indie/rock fans. So it was a result to go to a festival like that and go down so unexpectedly well – as opposed to the usual ones, where we know it will be a good show in front of a typical "Dread" crowd. The organisation was spot-on, with

quick changeovers not affecting a class monitor sound.'
**Greg Roberts (Dreadzone – Drums)**

'Normally we had another vocalist, Earl16, but this was one of the first gigs that I had to go up and sing some of his songs like "Once Upon A Time", "Little Britain", "Zion Youth" and stuff like that, which people know that he sings. But I jumped straight up on it and the crowd were wicked. A friend of mine came to Reading for the "Rock", so he sent me some text and he's over six foot, big guy, blonde hair in a ponytail, looks like Thor – and as I look round the corner, he's standing there, eyeballs rolling. and he'd got third degree sunburn on the Friday afternoon and had to go home straight after the gig. So, he said to me "all I remember about Reading is watching you, fucking peeling and getting in an ambulance!!!!" At 4:30pm in the afternoon... the tent jumping, and them accepting the fact that I wasn't an old-school reggae Jamaican Rastafarian, but a six-foot-six, bald-headed skinny South Londoner jumping about.'
**MC Spee (Dreadzone – Vocals)**

'I remember the enclosure; we were right next to the main stage and we could look out of our window... but we couldn't see the bands. Maggot dressed up once as Dick Turpin, I think Dan Tracey came on as Superman, he had no shoes on and ran right across the stage, and no one knew what the fuck was going on, of course. It changed my life.'
**P Xain (Goldie Lookin' Chain – Vocals)**

'Reading festival, fantastic. I like the policy of moving us once up the bill every year. We've worked out by the time 2014 comes along we'll be headlining.'
**Billy Webb (Goldie Lookin' Chain – Vocals)**

'I had never even been on a festival ground like that. It was first time really experiencing a festival at all, much less actually playing one. I'm not sure how many people were at the *NME* stage when we played at, I guess, 3 o'clock in the afternoon, but it seemed gigantic. I remember feeling a real sense of disassociation with the actual performance, because up until then our mode had always been to play to 200-300 capacity clubs and we'd got pretty good at doing that!! It definitely was a matter of thrusting us into a totally different arena of performance!!'
**Keith Murray (We Are Scientists – Vocals/Guitar)**

'We rushed on stage in front of the biggest audience we'd ever played to, and ripped through our set in kind of a daze.

It was wild to see so many kids jumping and singing and shouting, and it kind of made us think "wow, this is how it could be." We stayed around afterward and got to see a bunch of other amazing bands for the first time, including Arctic Monkeys, Arcade Fire, Babyshambles, and were especially psyched to see the Pixies, who are huge heroes of ours.'
**Michael Tapper (We Are Scientists – Drums)**

'I remember Sharin told me that she saw the Arcade Fire and they were just incredible. I don't have any recollection of seeing any bands that year; too busy partying after a tremendous gig. People sometimes say that great music makes for a great festival, but I believe that a great crowd of enthusiastic people makes for a great festival.'
**Sune Rose Wagner (The Raveonettes – Vocals/Guitar)**

'My job as compere at Reading has been a strangely enjoyable one. It started off on the Radio One stage with Bethan Elfyn and when Steve Lamacq decided he didn't want to do the main stage anymore, I got a call asking if I'd like to do it. Of course, nobody leaves a festival going "what a wonderful weekend of live music, but what was the compere on about?!" – it's the last thing on everyone's mind. But it's nice to give a band a big welcome onstage if they want one. Some bands have intro tapes themselves of course, and you get into a bit of a dizzy nervous wreck, only to be told by Chalkie the stage manager "no intro Huw".... I thought it'd be fun to take a snap of Marilyn Manson, but his private security man, a giant bloke, thought otherwise and took it off me. Every time the Foo Fighters play, the entire backstage bit is full of fans, friends and family, with everyone buzzing.'
**Huw Stephens (Main stage compere)**

'It was weird playing Reading, because I come from Reading and I grew up there as a kid. It was the highlight of the year since I was 16 and we'd camp out and get threatened by the locals. There used to be a bloke called Whitley John who walked around the campsite just terrorising people, he's quite famous actually in Reading as an absolute schitzo. He'd just nick people's tents and smash them up. I just associate it with being young and I never imagined I'd actually end up playing there. I don't think the third stage actually existed, which was where we played – there was only two of them, and a really tiny one. It was good, it was the first time that we tried our "backing singers", I don't really think of them as "backing singers", more like a gang of girls on stage shouting and doing high kicks. It was quite interesting, as these girls had never heard of the Reading Festival before, our manager found

*A fine figure of a man – Iggy commands the crowds from the stage*

them in a park in Stoke Newington doing handstands and stuff. Notting Hill falls on the same weekend as Reading and all these girls would have normally gone there and when they turned up they thought it was like a community festival and they hadn't any idea that they would be playing in front of 15,000.'
**Ian Parton (The Go! Team – Guitar/Harmonica/Drums)**

'I had never been to the festival before, but lots of my friends had been and had told me stories of Nirvana, LSD, urine, Hole, policemen, Lemonheads, and bruises, so I'd always been keen to attend.

'We didn't really do anything different for the festival show than we would do at the small club gigs we had been used to playing. Big festival gestures were never part of our plan. Although I do remember on the last chord of the last song lobbing my lovely new Gretsch guitar twenty foot into the air. I wasn't sure whether it was due to adrenaline or a brief moment of rock star fever but I missed catching it on it's return to earth and ended up trying to break the guitar's fall with my foot and thus ended up with a broken guitar and a badly bruised ankle.'
**Sam Forrest (Nine Black Alps – Vocals/Guitar)**

'The bouncers are all pretty strict and they've all got a bit of an attitude, they keep asking "WHERE'S YOUR PASS???" and you have to show it to them. I remember this because me and my girlfriend were trying to go to the shower and they were asking where we were going and I said "you don't really need to know, do you?" We had a pass with AAA and my girlfriend said that she needed a shower and he said "Are you taking your boyfriend with you????" Not everyone's like that, apparently!'
**Josh Morgan (The Subways – Drums)**

'The Wedding Present's modest van returned to the car park of the Reading Festival main stage after an absence of nine years to be sandwiched once more between huge sleeper buses and articulated lorries. Our little vehicle's section looked tiny on the parking plan, which I'm sort of proud of, if the truth be known. As soon as bands get the tiniest whiff of success the list of their whiny popstarry demands explodes. They suddenly need five star hotels, posh buses, legions of support crew, enough musical equipment to fill a warehouse and enough food and drink to feed an army. And the music they play is inevitably not as good as it used to be when they toured the country in the back of a transit van.
This year our set was the most varied selection we'd ever played at a Reading, with songs pulled from throughout the 20 years that we've been releasing records. Our guitarist,

Simon Cleave, put together this particular running order, and he obviously didn't do too bad a job because Radio One's Colin Murphy said that ours was his favourite set of the day.

'Throughout the hordes of skinny teenagers you could clearly pick out the Wedding Present fans... slightly older looking, slightly portlier, slightly balding... but still dancing around and seemingly enjoying themselves as much as they did at Reading 1989. And that was heartening to see!'
**David Gedge (The Wedding Present – Vocals/Guitar)**

'We played Leeds on the Friday and got there on the Saturday night. I think Arcade Fire was playing the Radio One Tent and Razorlight was on the main stage and we were in guest camping and we just heard this horrendous mix of both. I find Reading really weird generally, because the backstage area is this horrific amalgamation of the entire music industry. We've only ever played Reading on the Sunday, so by the time we get there it looks like a battle's been going on for about a week!'
**Whiskas (¡Forward Russia!) – Guitar)**

'Reading is still all about the music. Still rock'n'roll. The location is pretty cool, the layout is still very good and the backstage is still lively and very close to the stage, so you can get out and see stuff. It's always been a good party atmosphere backstage, there are always good big bars and it's just a really good site, a big field which you put music and 60,000 music fans in, which to us is what a festival is all about. We were really keen to do it and to play to all those people who'd never seen us before. Hopefully they will come back and see us again!! But it did in the end still feel like a Maiden show, with the great reaction the fans gave us.'
**Rod Smallwood (Chairman –
Sanctuary Artist Management)**

'We opened the main stage and that show marked my first experience of stage fright. I was gripping the drum sticks so hard my arms cramped up after the first song. By the time I relaxed and started having fun, the set ended. I never imagined that a hardcore band I started in my mom's garage would be on the main stage at perhaps the biggest festival in the world. Then we watched the Foo Fighters play to a bigger crowd than I can comprehend.'
**Francis Mark (From Autumn To Ashes – Drums/Vocals)**

'I played with British Sea Power, whose drummer was injured... I was attacked by a 14-foot bear in the last song, which perhaps displays the difference between the two bands

perfectly...Gene – Glitter/ BSP – 14-foot bear!!'
**Matt James (British Sea Power – Drummer)**

'We showed up at the press tent to do our interviews for the day. We were all trashed, and really just wanted to go hang out, maybe spot Dave Grohl. Either way, we do a couple interviews, and are ready to get it all over with. Finally, a beautiful woman in a bikini strolls over and sits between Bryan and I and starts taking off her few articles of clothing. Long story short, the naked interview ended far too soon, and she never ended up calling me.'
**Mat Barber (Emanuel – Guitar/Vocals)**

'I saw loads of people walking around barefoot, drinking and smoking first thing in the morning. It's just like this debauched

space in time where you turn up and do whatever and no one gives a fuck!'
**William Rees (Mystery Jets – Guitar/ Vocals/Percussion/Keyboards)**

'The best thing was that it secured the fact that we don't play in front of ten people anymore. To see all those people there, watching our band, it was absolutely fucking incredible! It was awesome, that was what we wanted to do all our lives – and free beer!!'
**Michael 'Padge' Padget (Bullet for My Valentine – Guitar/Vocals)**

'I recently had the pleasure of joining Harold Pendleton and his wife Barbara to celebrate his 80th birthday on a Thames cruise past his beloved festival site in Reading. And in the 2001

**Behind the Main Stage**

**The view from the half-built stage**

election, Harold put his personal political beliefs to one side and spent General Election day in my Reading West constituency, knocking on doors to help me get re-elected. Who said music and politics don't mix? They clearly do, and it is the reason we've still got a Reading Festival.'
**Martin Salter (Labour MP for Reading West)**

'With luminaries like the Foo Fighters and Bad Religion by the side of the stage we offered up our brand of American punk rock, fast, loud, obnoxious and incendiary. And there was plenty of full frontal male nudity from HeWhoCanNotBeNamed, the best looking man in show business. Afterwards, dozens of English girls insisted on sleeping with us and ingesting trendy London club drugs. Can you blame them?'
**Blag the Ripper (The Dwarves – Vocals)**

'The festival seemed pretty rubbish from a punter's point of view. I thought the food, beer and tickets were ridiculously overpriced and there were only one or two bands playing that seemed any good. The whole thing felt horribly corporate and sterile. I thought we played okay though.'
**Tom Shotton (Do Me Bad Things – Drums)**

'After getting all the right credentials tracked down, I headed out on a day of shooting. First up was Dinosaur Jr. Being on stage with them for that moment was great. It might have been the one show where Jay's guitar could have even been a LITTLE bit louder. A quick run down the backstage metal and mud trail to the tent where the Arcade Fire were set to go on. I was lucky enough to capture the camaraderie between this band. It's a group of really good friends and family who are passionate about the music and each other. Now came time for the Foos! I've shot with them the most out of any band and being around them and their crew is like being at a barbeque with some good friends and family. Nate is sitting in the doorway of the trailer with his son at his feet playing with a guitar pick. Dave and Jordan share laughs as Taylor talks about the festival's "jammy jam" cookies they have.

'Minutes before showtime they clear everyone out of the area so the band can prepare to go on stage. I'm lucky enough to be able to hang out and shoot photos. Dave turns up the Led Zep and pours a drink, pacing back and fourth in the trailer, warming up for the enormous crowd that's waiting. Taylor is drumming on the table with such concentration he is oblivious to me taking his photo. As the Foos finally take to the stage, the crowd goes insane. Never had I shot the group in front of this many people.

'This weekend cemented the fact that the Foo Fighters ARE one of the world's biggest and best rock bands.'
**Brantley Gutierrez (Photographer)**

'There weren't too many bands I wanted to see that day except the Pixies. I had been wanting to see them for ages. I entered the fest with ten friends and by the time the sun went down and the Pixies came on I was alone. Luckily, I met a cute pink-haired girl who watched in awe with me and kept me warm. After the Pixies, the pink haired bird and me went back to her tent and it was pure chaos everywhere. It was the perfect example of sex, drugs and rock 'n' roll. It was a very memorable experience for me.'
**Mick Morris (Eighteen Visions – Bass)**

'One clear and lasting memory of playing was meeting two young women who introduced themselves as the daughters of two of my most honoured and revered British musicians, from one of the best bands of all time. These two men, one dead and one still living (and producing great current British music) are probably among the most influential songwriters in my life and yours.

'Talking to them was depressing, scary and interesting. You may be thinking: "These girls cannot be the daughters of these two great musicians." I thought the very same thing. But, there was something in their eyes and tone that made me believe them. They were, after all, telling us detailed descriptions of their home lives and were dead ringers for their respective dads. I am pretty sure they were the real deal. I am positive they were in trouble.

'Long story short, we did not have the drugs they wanted, or any interest in engaging them in their sex stories. They left after about 15 minutes to see the Foo Fighters.'
**Dave Walsh (The Explosion – Guitar)**

'My memory was seeing Arcade Fire from the side of the stage. I'd never seen them before, but I was pretty aware of their music. But because it was from the side of the stage, you don't get the full impact of the PA, so I was really focusing on the way they performed and moved in and out of eachother, swapping instruments.

'I mainly remember Richard Reed Parry, who's known as "dude in the crash helmet" and he's apparently one of the geniuses behind the band. He was hitting everything in sight with his drumsticks, including his own crash helmet. Then he went up to the rigging, which was pretty much where I was standing, and started battering the rigging. It was a pretty physical performance.'
**Jamie Ellis (Battle – Guitar)**

'My girlfriend was very drunk, so I had to look after her. We went back to her tent to pick up all of her stuff. We were sitting in the tent having a cuddle, not doing anything rude and all of a sudden we heard this noise, like "WOOOAARRGGHHH!" It was getting louder and louder, it was quite scary, lots of blokes and lots of girls all shouting.

'I looked out of the tent and saw a bloke in a gorilla suit run past going "AAAARRRRGGGGGGHHHHHH!!!!" Then, about a minute later, I saw about a hundred people chasing him!'
**Oliver Davies (Battle – Drums)**

'The gig itself was a weird experience. Having strolled about watching bands, gawping at old heroes backstage, it was strange being one of the performers. Like I said, it was our first time playing Reading, and I had gotten fully in to the mode of being a festival goer, not part of a band. It all seemed to be over in about ten seconds. Ten very good seconds, but ten seconds nonetheless. Which basically means we had a lot of fun!'
**Espen Dahl (The Cherubs – Guitar)**

'I did my new act "The Great Voltini's Electrocution Show" for the late-night cabaret. Before I went on there were two east-European girls singing something arty and the crowd hated them, insults and bottles of water reigning down nineteen to the dozen. Not the best atmosphere to do a show using live, high voltage machines.

'The compere managed to calm the crowd enough so I could set the props. I was introduced and before I'd even said a word the first bottle hit the stage. At this point my voluptuous and very sweet looking assistant, Nurse Electra, lost her rag and yelled at the top of her voice (this is in a packed tent full of thousands of noisy, drunken revellers and without a microphone) "If you don't fucking pack it in we're not fucking doing it!!"'

'The stunned crowd let out a huge cheer, and from then on the show worked a treat.'
**Bastard Son of Tommy Cooper (Magician)**

'I specialise in Twisted Neo Burlesque Cabaret. Taking this style of entertainment to the masses can be a risky business! "Get ya kit off" seems to be the favourite heckle, for those fortunate enough to have front row viewing. Luckily for me, I invariably do get my kit off, that is if I was wearing anything in the first place.

'The audience is tough, they have been drinking and dancing all day, they want to see some action and I love to give it to them. My infamous "Diamond Pussy" act is a sure fire hit (that's when I pull a string of Diamonds out of my Pussy), the Rose Eating and Blood Drinking gets the vote and when I pull a gold balloon out of my arse and pop it in a cloud of glitter... Well, nobody is throwing bottles at the stage.'
**Empress Stah (Burlesque Cabaret performer)**

'I'm 38 now and still a huge music fan. However, each year Reading crowds seem to be getting younger. Mind you, so do policemen. Sometimes whilst roaming around the site I get the impression that I must look like a concerned father who's lost his daughters and has his Volvo parked on yellow lines outside. Young people at Reading like to make small, rather token, fires with empty beer cups. Because these cups are coated in some form of plastic, the resulting (and I'm sure fairly toxic) odour is an ever present irritant around the site when the sun goes down... but then again, as I said before, I'm 38 and I'm perhaps more suited to Glastonbury and its real wood fires stoked by whacked-out hippies who live in horseboxes and make their own shoes.'
**Ben Norris (Comedian)**

'The annual event at the Rivermead Leisure Centre in Richfield Avenue is one of the biggest occasions of the year in the borough. It is licensed to host 66,500 people, including guests, and around 40,000 of these will be weekend campers. A police station, complete with staff to record crimes, a front counter service, interview teams and rooms, and prisoner holding areas will be on the site. Officers will also be providing high profile patrol in areas to prevent thefts from tents, violence and robberies. They will be supported by security staff employed by the Mean Fiddler.

'Chief Inspector Steve Thwaites, who heads Operations at Berkshire West, and has overseen the planning of the event, said: "Considering the huge number of people who come to the festival, it is usually a peaceful and well-organised event, where a good time is had by all – even in appalling weather conditions. However, with such a large gathering of people comes an opportunity that, for many, is too good to miss and every year there are the same issues, with people having goods stolen from their tents or going to other parts of Reading and falling victim of crime. My message to the local offenders who see the festival as easy pickings is that we have our eyes on them. All staff receive briefing packs and we will be stopping and challenging people. This approach led to no robberies at WOMAD and we want to repeat that at Reading.'
**Thames Valley Police**

'I have to say right away that I have never appeared at the Reading Festival either as a performer or a spectator, so what I could add to your first-hand experiences from inside the arena is, quite frankly, nil. However, even though I'm bearing down on my 60th birthday, I've always been a supporter of the festival and one day (when I'm not otherwise occupied at the time) I do hope to attend.'
**Clive Ormonde (Map – Reading)**

'The Reading Festival is a bit of a beast. Being an "alt-Americana" band, we were a little surprised how well we went down, which is a testament to the fact that it's not only the usual suspects that work at festivals, but an open approach to music genres....'
**Jason Moffat (The Cedars – Guitar/Banjo)**

'Our project was devised at one Reading Festival a few years back, when the organisers forgot to put up viewing platforms, and there were no accessible toilets and all the disabled customers went and complained en masse to the box office. There were many festival-goers and festival staff alike who were pretty taken aback by the ferocity of the mini riot! However, it did the trick, because I'm proud to say that 10 years later, Carling Weekend: Reading Festival is now held up as an example of Best Practice in accessibility to other festivals.'
**Suzanne Bull (Attitude is Everything Project Manager)**
www.attitudeiseverything.org.uk

Black Francis of the Pixies contemplates
his future, during their headline set

# 2006

The headliners consisted of two bands who had worked their way up the bill and one legend. Franz Ferdinand had played the Carling tent in '03, the main stage in '04, and deservedly headlined this year. The same could be said for Muse, with appearances in '99, '00 and '02. Pearl Jam were making a rare festival appearance, their first since the Roskilde disaster in 2000 and the only 'full Pearl Jam' show at Reading – having appeared as a backing band for Neil Young in 1995. Sunday saw Slayer debut and My Chemical Romance overcome the constant pelting (even golf balls), to perform a set that gained them many fans and the appreciation of the crowd.

'We'd been away for a while that year so it was great to come back on the main stage. We played five new songs from the album and it was one of the first times we played "Angry Mob". It was quite daring to play new songs, but they went down well. We had the massive "KC" which looked great; we wanted to do something good, but to keep it simple. Ryan from the Cribs came on with us as well, and it was the usual shambolic event.'
**Simon Rix (Kaiser Chiefs – Bass)**

'When we came to play we wanted to steal the show, so we tried to think that it was our festival and it did feel like we were headlining. I tend to see bands before we go on, to get in the right frame of mind. To see the crowd is quite important.'
**Nick Hodgson (Kaiser Chiefs – Drums/Vocals)**

'Reading '06 for YYYs was especially splendid and theatrical. We rolled with a small army, clones included. First off, it felt really good to slap a grown man dressed up as me while thousands watched on the jumbo screen. I was a little disappointed afterward to find out my Karen O lookalike much rather would dress up as Princess Di than a beer-dribbling rockette.... Also our Reading set had a rather anti-climactic end when I decided to roll around in the wood chips below the stage, kicking sawdust in the faces of the kindly security men and women who were only there to protect me. Alas, Godzilla made me do it.'
**Karen O (Yeah Yeah Yeahs – Vocals)**

'The show itself was awesome and ridiculous. Earlier Brendan from Panic! At The Disco got hit with a bottle, so we decided we were going to get the crowd to throw trash at each other! I remember looking and you could see trash flying and you couldn't see out at all, that was cool. There were kids singing along to all the words and it was really hot.'
**Pete Wentz (Fall Out Boy – Bass)**

'We've all been to the festival as punters in the past, and it was always the main stage where the large-scale theatrics

would take place. Walking out onto that stage this year... I defy any band that has played the main stage to not be moved by the scene  so many people! The crowd are there to be part of something. The band want to create something special. It's in the air. Everyone is working together to create something legendary. It's much more than just a show. There's an immediate link between the crowd and the band  a willingness to create something special.  Playing "Hounds of Love" and "He Knows" and having the crowd sing, scream and clap back it's unforgettable.'
**Ross Millard (The Futureheads – Vocals/Guitar)**

'I've got about six or seven years of physically being at Reading, basically through working at MTV. I'd always heard about it and had these preconceptions of it being a "heavy rock" festival, but it has transformed from its early jazz roots and reinvented itself. It's never snobbish about music and it gives you the chances to not only see legends like Pearl Jam but also introduces you to so many new bands as well. I remember seeing Keane for the first time in the Carling Tent and there were maybe 20 people watching them, so that is testament to why Reading is so important to introducing you to new music.

'It's very much a music fans' festival - look at the size of the crowd that Panic! At The Disco drew at two o'clock in the afternoon. Reading is just about the music and people will get up to come and see the bands they want to see and they will wander around the tents and still party hard.'
**Edith Bowman (Radio One DJ)**

'It was a great day and there were a lot of people there. The crowd were crazy and they enjoyed it very much. I also played with Franz Ferdinand, who got a bunch of drummers onstage, about eight or nine of the main stage drummers who had played that day and it was very tribal and exciting. It was definitely worth it because the crowd loved it.'
**Josh Morgan (The Subways – Drums)**

Ricky Wilson of Kaiser
Chiefs screams from the
Main Stage

'It's an awesome festival with a great history, and both times we've had such an incredible response – the crowd's energy was over the top! The fans are so passionate and supportive. It's one of the great festivals in the world, without a doubt (with arguably the best VIP tent, too).'
**Claudio Sanchez (Coheed And Cambria – Vocals/Guitar)**

'It was a great crowd and I told them that I had pissed in the dad's assholes, which went down well.'
**Adam Dutkiewicz (Killswitch Engage – Guitar)**

'It was a great show, the kids were really keen, and it was just great to play here.'
**Howard Jones (Killswitch Engage – Vocals)**

'Every Reading I've played, I just got more comfortable, so the last time if I was really shit I don't care, and I'm just here to have a good time... I'm kinda happy to be there, because there are always bands that I want to see at Reading. Whether they're big bands, to see how cheesy they are, or really small bands to see how great they are.'
**Lou Barlow (Dinosaur Jr – Bass)**

'It was a huge stage, a big crowd, everything sounded good, and it was just so much fun getting to play our music to so many people. There were a few kids throwing bottles and cake and stuff, but there always is. But I think we dealt with that, we just dodged them and we moved around a lot.'
**Angel Ibarra (Aiden – Guitar)**

'The show was good, but it was so quiet with the volume control in the tent. Ice-T was playing and a guy decided to play a trick on him and dressed up as a donkey or in a horse suit or something. Ice-T didn't have a sense of humour! It was the most out-of-the-ordinary event that day!!'
**Gregg Attonito (Bouncing Souls – Vocals)**

'I remember getting into trouble with Boysetsfire. It's a just a big gathering and it's something I always look forward to.'
**Bryan 'Papillon' Kienlen (Bouncing Souls – Bass)**

'Body Count and Ice-T, I won't forget their drum solo ever! You walk around in the mud and see all these bands.... The excitement level in Europe is so much better than anything in the States. In the UK there are so many festivals, but they are all so amazing.'
**Michael 'Madman' McDermott
(Bouncing Souls – Drums)**

'We had been on the Warped tour with Rise Against and Thursday. We'd just got home for about a week, and then all the same bands turned up at Reading, which was cool.'
**Pete 'The Pete' Steinkopf (Bouncing Souls – Guitar)**

'When me and Jamie were both teenagers and all of the kids in the same classes as us were going off to all the major festivals at summertime and coming back with these incredible mythical encounters of whirlwind drugs binges and illicit encounters under soggy sleeping bags with famous rockstars, we vowed to NEVER go these festivals unless we had a band and a gig there. Of course we grew up in separate parts of the country at slightly different times but in 2006 we had been in a band called the Noisettes together for two years and we finally got a chance to play the Carling stage at Reading and Leeds.... One weird thing about playing at both festivals is wherever you were on the running order for Saturday in Reading, you'd be in the same position in Leeds the next day. You can then imagine the feelings of deja vu when we'd just played Leeds the second day and yet again, as I walked into catering to get my food, I hear Feeder (ironically) playing the same song they were playing the moment I was doing exactly the same thing yesterday in a place that looks EXACTLY THE SAME!'
**Dan Smith (The Noisettes – Vocals/Guitar)**

'It was our first experience of playing a British festival. Reading was a very important festival to do, as I went first when I was 16. It was always the festival that I associated with my teens and so it was pretty nerve-wracking to play it. We somehow managed to get a decent slot and on a decent stage – quite a mystery to us how we pulled that off! There was a big crowd, no one left and it went off without incident. We got really drunk and I was supposed to DJ in the backstage VIP bar, but I really was too drunk. It was also very memorable for our bass player Matty, who paraded around the backstage area in a pair of green velour hot pants. I don't quite know why, but I'd put it down to the beer and the sun!'
**Nick Peill (Fields – Vocals/Acoustic Guitar/Keyboards)**

'Our neighbours in the portakabins were Primal Scream, which was weird. The catering was particularly nice, chicken with parmesan and spaghetti. Because it was such nice weather it made the festival that much better. Hanging around in the VIP bar it was great to just people-watch. We caught up with Zane Low, and at one point saw Ice-T and Kelly Osborne. The DJing experience was quite entertaining as well in the VIP bar, but we weren't really told when it was going to be, so we

had to hurriedly put together a couple of mix cds on Nick's computer. We'd assumed it would have been in the afternoon, so we put together a chilled-out set and it ended up that we went on at 11pm, after someone had been dropping lots of techno! The dance floor cleared in about two seconds. So we had to quickly find anything that would get the dance floor moving, even Whitney Houston!'
**Jamie Putnam (Fields – Guitar)**

'When we found out that we'd got Reading it was great, as we had a really good slot. We tried to play with passion, love and appreciation for the people who had made the effort to get out of bed at noon and come and see us – and there were a lot of people. I had a friend say after the show "let's go and see this band Klaxons". It was like actually getting to be back in the civilian world, instead of in a backstage reality. It was great to see how excited the crowd was and my friend and I pushed right into the centre of the audience, which was really wild and it helped me remember what it is to go to festivals and stay on the right side of the music and remember to be a fan of music.'
**Emily Haines (Metric – Vocals/Synthesizer)**

'Just getting the email and being asked... we'd been excited all summer, because we don't even normally get to go because we're so skint. As soon as we found out we were playing, we decided we'd go down on the Thursday night, do some partying in the VIP area and just enjoy everything... and we didn't actually sleep much all weekend. I was surprised I could actually sing when it got to the Saturday because so much had happened up to that point. It was our best gig ever and we've done over 600!'
**Jamie Searle (Adequate Seven – Vocals)**

'We came on the Thursday. Two of our friends thought they would go up on stage when Ice-T and Bodycount were playing, as he has a bit of a rep as being a "gangsta". So they were backstage and had this pantomime horse costume and the stage manager told them that there was no way they were getting up on stage like that. But as soon as his back was turned they ran up there in this horse costume. Bodycount had stopped playing and it was in between songs and suddenly this horse was up there trotting across the stage. Ice-T and Bodycount were there, arms folded, seriously pissed off... They were these crazy guys from Derby and a great band

**169**

**Arctic Monkeys sing to the crowd as the sun goes down**

and lovely people, but they'd ruined Bodycount's weekend. They then came off stage and Bodycount's manager and the stage manager were having a massive go at them and they ran off and were being chased by Bodycount's tour manager and they decided to go into the *NME* tent. The stage manager was there and said "What are you doing" and they said "Our friend wants us to go on stage" and he said "Who's your friend" and they looked across and Dizzy Rascal was standing there, so they said it was him. So the stage manager said "you'll have to ask him". So, this pantomime horse goes up to Dizzy Rascal and says "You've got to help us. Ice-T is trying to kill us". And he said "No mate. No mate!!!"

**Gavin Fitzjohn (Adequate Seven – Trumpet)**

'For me it was really special, because when you're a kid the highlight of every year is going down to Reading with all of your mates and discovering what you're into, like a "coming of age". It's like a highlight of the summer, and then when you hear that you're playing it, it's every band's dream... I personally didn't expect as good a reaction as we had.'

**Kassim D Basma (Adequate Seven – Guitar)**

'Fifteen minutes before I went on there were people spilling out of the tent, about ten rows out, and I had people texting me saying "we can't get into the tents, it's heaving!" It was absolutely fantastic, from the first song onwards the atmosphere was insane. It was a marker point in my career to gauging that things were really starting to kick off.'

**Sam Duckworth AKA Get Cape, Wear Cape, Fly (Vocals/Guitar)**

'The whole place seems quite mental. We got no soundcheck, so we just had to walk in and get on with it. The gig itself was great, just seeing the people coming in to check us out in a 10,000 capacity tent, you want it to be full, but you don't expect it.'

**MC Lord Magrão (Guillemots – Guitar)**

The monitors weren't brilliant! It was one of our biggest shows, but we played faster than normal. I guess it was the nerves kicking in, but it sounded like the Clash playing Guillemots songs. It was quite raucous. We did an acoustic show in the Tiscali tent and made up instruments as we didn't expect to do it. I played water bottles and MC Lord Magrão played a typewriter!'

**Greig Stewart (Guillemots – Drums)**

'I was woken up two hours before the show by our tour manager. I got up out of my bunk and traipsed around the bus, trying to work out where the hell I was. Wandered out and had some food and then had a shower in the portable shower with three people knocking on the door to see if anyone was in there. Came and had half an hour to get on stage, put on some t-shirts from the last few shows, had a vodka and Red Bull and went on stage. We played with a lot of energy and it all kinda rolled along pretty well.'

**Andrew Stockdale (Wolfmother – Vocals/Guitar)**

'As far as I know we are the only band that has gone Carling stage, *NME* stage and main stage in three consecutive years. Going to the main stage was easy, as we have been working up to it, but to finally do it was good.

'It's something that I've always wanted to do. I've been coming here since I was 16 at high school. I came here pretty much every year since. Halfway through the set the sun came out, which was really nice, but on the Friday night I sang a song with the Kaiser Chiefs and it were proper pissing it down. I've never seen it so bad.'

**Ryan Jarman (The Cribs – Vocals/Guitar)**

'2006 was one of the best ever; hoggin' the backstage ping pong table from Panic At The Disco, Beach Ball fighting at the Fratellis Carling Show, Peaches' inflatable phallus stretchered off stage, meeting Jack White (however briefly), and seeing Paul Smith of Maximo Park serenading a pot of hummus with Pearl Jam numbers. But the outstanding memory over and above all the years at the festival was DJing with Steve Lamacq at the Silent Disco.

'Picture the scene. The Raconteurs have just performed an earth-shattering set, small cranes are fixing up fences before the stage, Dutch DJs called "Shdevie" are on the microphone "shomeone has asked for Britney, the shimple anshwer is No!", and a couple of thousand party happy people singing along to every word, despite the music being heard – that's right – through only headphones. The night became more and more surreal as the Raconteurs, Goldie Lookin Chain, *NME* hacks and random crew members join us on stage, throwing shapes to invisible tunes, culminating in King Pengelly (the man who books all the festival bands), dancing on the speakers, gyrating away. This is the funniest, stoopidest thing I have ever seen at Reading. This was the "roll" to the day's "rock", and was the absolute antithesis of the "this band is my life" seriousness of thousands of us staring up for hours on end at the rock monsters of our day. This was Reading turned on its head, a karaoke of chaos, and another body breaking night out!'

**Bethan Elfyn (BBC Radio One Presenter/DJ/ Compere)**

'It's a mini-city of all things music, mostly rock, some pop and emo as well as the random novelty act, to bring a shimmering smile to your face. Driving into the otherwise ordinary town of Reading, thousands of kids are frantically following the golden signs, turning this town into a kind of Xanadu for three days. Selling tickets, buying tickets, screaming, pushing, laughing, dancing, some are asleep on the side of the road having not been so lucky this year….they know there's always next year. But most are preparing themselves for a weekend of unrelenting rock'n'roll….clearly the stuff teenage dreams are made of!

'As Lady Luck would have it, we were on at the same time as The Vines and Yeah Yeah Yeahs… GRRRRRR… the two bands I was most looking forward to seeing over the next couple days. Oh well, the show must go on, and it did. Made way for Eagles of Death Metal, who were really cool. Lead singer told me he wasn't worried about the audience cos they "fucking worship my ass anyway". I laughed.
**Juanita Stein (Howling Bells – Vocals)**

'At the outdoor festivals in the States, we've never played a stage in a big tent, so it was a new experience for us. The experience was sort of the best of both worlds, large crowds, but there was the intimacy of a club and we had lights and the PA didn't sound like crap from the wind. We went on and the crowd was electric. I don't really recall much about the performance other then the crowd being great.

'Perhaps the most memorable experience next to taking an ice-cold shower in a trailer (we don't have trailer showers at US festivals) was watching Muse perform later that evening while standing in the middle of the mud field. I was absolutely blown away by their stage show. They had these massive LED backdrops that moved all over the place. By far the best light show I've ever seen. It was the highlight of my Reading experience.'
**Eron Bucciarelli (Hawthorne Heights – Drums)**

'Nice to see 747s fans had come that early. We all had a brandy ration and went up there and gave it our all. It was a great show. The crowd reaction was super and the feedback after the show was really great. It fell like our first proper festival performance.

'I remember hands in the air clapping along to our song "Rainkiss"; the crowd were in good spirit at the start of a long day. It will be a memory that will stay with me for life, standing on the side of the stage watching the Arctic Monkeys play. They seemed to woo over the crowd effortlessly. Afterwards, I remember Alex Turner telling me that it seemed really quiet from where he was on the stage. Kind of a weird silence. When the Arctic Monkeys played "Leave Before The Lights Go Out" I remember thinking that this is just glorious. They brought that song to life. The recording of the song is very good but live they took it elsewhere.'
**Oisin Leech (747s – Vocals/Bass)**

'We went to Reading the day before we played, watched Primal Scream from the side of the stage and danced our asses off. When we played Reading it was fun, backstage Giant Drag were there and all our crazy friends were there on the side of the stage. We were relatively tame when we were at Reading, wandering around the grassy field in our little dresses and the crew members backstage were like "are they groupies?"

During the Arctic Monkeys we went into the crowd with a couple of friends, and as we were leaving the audience one of my friends felt something warm on her feet, this man had decided to relieve himself on her. She is French and she was like "WHAT ARE YOU DOING?" She grabbed his beer off him and threw it into his face, but that's French models for you!!!'
**Elizabeth 'Z' Berg (The Like – Vocals/Guitar)**
**Charlotte Froom (The Like – Bass/Vocals)**
**Tennessee Thomas (The Like – Drums/Vocals)**

'I played drums with Franz Ferdinand, in front of 60,000 people.'
**Gareth Jennings (Mumm-Ra – Drums)**

'I was wandering around after the Franz Ferdinand set getting dumped on with buckets of rain, all of my friends having peeled off a few songs past. So I'm drunk with "fuck-it" pretty much written on my face, and I come across a group of Scottish blokes huddled around a fire that they had hastily constructed out of discarded paper pint cups. And they are playing a game. As far as I could tell the name of the game was "Who can keep their hands over the fire the longest."'
**James Krimmel (Scissors For Lefty – Bass/Drums)**

'For the price of a cup of tea indeed! I'm trying to put together a decent cup of tea and who should steal the sugar out from under me but Stuart from Belle and Sebastian. That pretty much sums up the surreal turn that normal daily activities would take at the Reading Festival. Wait in line at the artist hospitality tent for your daily bread, only to find that some dude from Panic At The Disco's taken the last biscuit. Not that anyone's complaining.'

**Peter Krimmel (Scissors For Lefty – Keyboard/Guitar)**

'What will I remember most at Reading Festival?? Easy. Come now, let's stutter together. Everybody say "yeah!" Come on now, say "yeah!!" Now, let's make it plural. Say, "Yeahs!!!" What's that spell?? Err, I dunno. How many pints has your soundman had, hmm?? Ah, that's nothing mate, our soundman had enough lager to pull his pants down, pick up our manager, sling her across his shoulders, and then take off sprinting around the festival grounds!!'

**Bryan Garza (Scissors For Lefty – Vocals/Guitar**

'We played the second slot on the Carling stage, which by the festival's standards is very early and very small, but the tent was nevertheless packed to the gills with a boisterous, teetering crowd, and felt enormous. The set was fun, the sound was big, and the audience was with us from the first note. Noon at Reading, it seems, is not too early to rock. There is a palpable and contagious energy in the air at that place; the feeling of 80,000 people simultaneously tuning out the world and committing to a sort of fairyland filled with music and mayhem. It's a blast.'

**Eli Miller (Zox – Guitar/Vocals)**

'This year we got an invite to the *Kerrang!* aftershow party on the Thursday, and got to the site to see the last bit of Fall Out Boy. My Chemical Romance turned the crowd round from being bottled at first to being loved (well not bottled) by the time they left.'

**Mike Horton (Festival Regular and Driver)**

'This year we ran the Love Not Riots Campaign, a peace movement to try and bring an end to the Sunday night violence and riots that Reading and Leeds have witnessed over the last few years. Love not Riots earned the support of several major bands and reached the ears of National Music Promotion Company Mean Fiddler, who helped us to make our campaign successful and thus their festival a safer environment for thousands of music lovers from around the UK that descend on The Carling Weekend every year....

We don't think that we encountered any negative comments about our campaign, every one saw the good in it, apart from Slayer at the signing tent, they just said "We like riots" but that we believe is just an image thing ... we reckon they are teddy

bear hugging softies really, Tee Hee! Muse were enthralling and we really didn't want them to stop and it was a superb experience seeing Eddie Vedder doing his thang and shedding a few post-set tears before leaving the stage! Then left with nothing but a field full of empty Carling cups we retreated to our camp site, wiping away solemn tears from our soggy faces, tripping over our droopy bottom lips at the terrifying thought of returning back to civilisation and the humdrum that is life and leaving behind for another 360 days the phenomenon that is ...the Reading Festival.'

**Zena Gardner & Amy (Love Not Riots – Campaign)**

'Booking for the following year usually starts in the bar of the Holiday Inn, Reading on the Sunday night of the festival and carries on right up to the week before the festival. Generally, headliners get booked before the end of January and then I work down the bills from there in as methodical way as this business allows. I try to keep the different days' bills as varied as possible and have the different stages complementing eachother whenever possible. Headliners are usually based on which big acts have albums out, or are touring, and bands that haven't headlined too recently. Melvin Benn, Denis Desmond and I try to reach a general consensus on the best bands to go for.

'I've been at Mean Fiddler for around 15 years now and been booking all the acts for Reading since '94, so there's been a lot of great performances in that time and to single out any would be unfair, so I'd say the best performance at Reading is the next one I'll see. That anticipation of seeing a band play a blinder (or spectacularly fuck up) is what it's all about.'
**Neil Pengelly (Mean Fiddler – Festival Booker)**

**The sun sets over Security...**

# 2007epilogue

With the return of the Chili Peppers for their third headline show, Smashing Pumpkins for their second and a debut bill topper for Razorlight, all is set for a fantastic weekend. With mainstage debuts from Maximo Park and Bloc Party, who have both headlined the Radio One stage, and the long-awaited festival return of Ash, the bill has never been stronger. All we can hope for now is nice weather and plenty of craziness....

# INDEX OF CONTRIBUTORS

## A

Aaron, Lee 76
Aldridge, Tommy 55
Allison, Dot 131
Andrew, Harvey 29
Andrew, W.K. 140
Attonito, Gregg 152, 168
Archer, Gem 128
Arentzen, Jamie 137
Attila the Stockbroker 85

## B

Baldes, Kevin 126
Banks, Peter 44
Barber, Chris 12
Barber, Mat 161
Barlow, Lou 107,168
Barr, Al 152
Barrett, Aaron 140
Bartlett, Jo 131
Basma, Kasim D 170
Bastard Son of Tommy
  Cooper 111,164
Bellamy, Tom 110
Belland, Tracey 83
Bonn, Molvin 7
Bentley, Mike 66
Berg, Elizabeth 'Z' 171
Bethan, Elfyn 170
Bevan, Bev 64
Birch, Joe 136,149
Bjork, Brant 121
Black Francis 86
Black, Frank 104
Blackwell, Nigel 86-88
Blade 137
Blag the Ripper 163
Bloom, Luka 88
Bobjack, Jim 80
Boobe 143
Boom, Sonic 85
Boon, Clint
  86,92,114,128
Bottum, Roddy 86
Bowen, Gene 106
Bowman, Edith 166
Bown, Andy 13
Box, Mick 79

Boyce, Keith 26
Bromham, Del 16,19
Brooks, Elkie 16,19
Brous, Raph 155
Brown, Arthur 13,14
Bucciarelli, Eron 171
Bull, Suzanne 164
Burchell, Jamie 144
Burnel, JJ 74
Burrows, Lee 49
Butler, Toby 155
Butt, Gizz 114
Byker, Mary 82

## C

Cairns, Andy 98, 100,104
Carter, Les 92
Cann, Warren 38, 42-44, 49
Carroll, Steve 49
Carson, Phil 30,36
Carter, Neil 50
Catskilkin, Ian 157
Chandler, Erik 131, 146
Chaos, Casey 131,136
Chappell, Marion 94
Chatton, Brian 19
Chevron, Philip 38, 82
Childish, Billy 148
Clayden, JS 126
Clemison, Zal 38
Clown #6 128
Collins, Andrew 102
Collister, Kim 111
Cooper, Alice 74
Coverdale, David 50
Cross, Chris 38
Cut La Roc 120

## D

Dahl, Espen 163
Davies, Oliver 163
Davis, Michael 152-54
de Offlicence, Robber 82
Derakh, Amir 72
Difford, Chris 45
Dorney, Tim 92
Dorset, Ray 19
Downick, Ade 133

Downing, KK 30
Duckworth, Sam 170
Dufort, Denise 56
Dumpy 30,70,76
Dunnery, Frank 72-73
Dutkiewicz, Adam 168
Dweeb, Kris 115,117

## E

Eero 154
Ellis, Jamie 163
Empire, Alex 124,143
Empress Stah 164

## F

Feldman, John 143,154
Ferguson, Lloyd 'Judge' 36
Fiddler, John 14
Fiorello, Vinnie 148
Fisher, Daniel 131
Fisher, John Norwood 101
Fitzgerald, Warren
  Anthony 126
Fitzjohn, Gavin 169-70
Flenniken, Brian 149
Ford, Joby 155
Forrest, Sam 160
Foxx, John 38,42
Franks, Simon 148
French, Jay Jay 61-62
Froom, Charlotte 171
Fujiyama, Yoshiko
'Ronnie' 155

## G

Gallant, Jon 146
Gambaccini, Paul 22
Gardner, Zena 172
Garza, Bryan 172
Gautrey, Ben 105, 131
Gedge, David
  82,86,104,124,160
George, Robin 51,56
Gentling, Matt 104
Gerald 53
Gibbs, Dave 100
Gillan, Ian 12,46,58,64
Ginger 106,152

Godley, Kevin 26
Goodwin, Jim 56,102,124
Gould, Billy 86
Gray, Paul 40
Greaves, Dennis 51-52, 58
Green, Adam 137
Gurney, Wol 144
Gutierrez, Brantley 163

## H

Hackett, Steve 22
Haigh, Kerstin 102
Haines, Emily 169
Hamill, Peter 36
Hamilton 148
Harding, John Wesley 55
Harley, Steve 26,66
Harper, John 114, 148
Harris, Andy 77
Harry 137
Harvey, Robert 140
Hawkins, Chris
  131,138,144
Hawkins, Taylor 140
Hayman, Darren 123
Helders, Matt 156
Henley, Des 22-24,28-29
Herrera, Mike 121
Hersh, Kristin 110
Hingley, Tom 86
Hodgson, Nick 166
Hodgson, Roger 30
Holden, John 117
Hood, Henri 85
Hooton, Peter 98
Horton, Mike 131,172
Hunt, Miles 78
Hussey, Wayne 70, 82, 98
Hyper Helen 122

## I

Ian Cognito 127
Ibarra, Angel 168

## J

James, Matt 108,160-61
Jarman, Ryan 170
Jenkins, Bill 53-55

Jennings, Gareth 171
Jim Bob 92,108
Jocz, Steve 148
John, Cat 155
John e. 115,138
Johnson, Kelly 56
Johnson, Les 78
Johnston, James 136
Jones, Danko 154
Jones, Howard 168
Joolz 84-85

## K

Kale, Paul 76
Karen 'O' 166
Kennemore, Phil 62
Kenney, Evan 154-55
Keuning, David 156
Khin, Greg 45
Kienlen, Bryan 'Papillon'
  168
King, Dave 155
King, Jem 144
Kirton, Mick 14,24,71,77
Klopfenstein, Scott 140
Koff, Rory 122
Kogan, Theo 99
Koller, Lou 124,143
Koller, Peter 124
Krimmel, James 171
Krimmel, Peter 171-72
Kulash, Damien 149
Kulick, Bob 79

## L

Laidlaw, Ray 16, 24-25
Lane, Corinne 111
Latimer, Andy 37
Lawton, John 38
Lay, Ed 166
Leary, Paul 83
Lee, Christopher 'Krasp'
  115
Leech, Oisin 171
Lewis, Juliette 157
Lewis, Mike 136
Lynton, Jackie 39
Lyons, Leo 13, 66

# M

Mack, Steve 94,98
McAuliffe, Kim 56
McAvoy, Gerry 14,34,50
McCabe, Zia 140
McCoy, John 31,45,47-49,51,58
McDermott, Michael 'Madman' 168
MacIntyre, Colin 137,146
MacManus, Davey 131
McManus, Pat 66
McMurray, Rick 112,134
McNamara, Danny 128
Magrao, MC Lord 170
Marklew, Leigh 105,124
Mark B 137
Mark, Francis 160
Marko 72 149
Marsden, Bernie 31,49,50,62
Marx, Gary 32,40
Mason, Steve 108
May, Brian 77
MC Spree 158
Mendoza, Mark 'The Animal' 62
Merrill, Alan 79
Michaelson, Nick 102
Miles, Kevin 105,108,136
Millard, Ross 166
Miller, Eli 172
Mindwarp, Zodiac 74
Moffat, Jason 166
Mogg, Nigel 80
Monkman, Francis 36
Monroe, Michael 66
Moody, Micky 12, 31,36,38,62
Moore, Angelo 101
Morgan, Josh 160,166
Morris, Mick 163
Morrison, Billy 138
Moses, Stephen 102
Murph 94
Murray, Keith 158
Murray, Pauline 45

# N

Navetta, Dan 149
Nawaz, Aki 107
Neabore, Dave 116
Norris, Ben 164
Nugent, Ted 35
Numan, Gary 134

# O

Ojeda, Eddie 62
Ormonde, Clive 164
O'Shea, Declan 124
Otway, John 79

# P

Padget, Michael 'Padge' 161
Parker, Graham 12,38,72
Parsons, Dave 45
Parton, Ian 158-60
Paskins, Paul 40
Pavanella, Paolo 138
Peck, Chris 157
Peill, Nick 168
Pengelly, Neil 172-73
Perrier, Ben 149
Polymorphic Spree, The 146
Porkbeast 84
Powell, Don 51
Preston 155
Princess Superstar 144
Putnam, Jamie 168-69

# Q

Quatro, Suzi 66

# R

Rarebell, Herman 46
Rasmussen, Brett 126
Reddick, Jaret 128-31,146
Rees, William 161
Regan, Bridget 155
Regan, Dan 152
Riley, George 154
Riley, Marc 96
Riley, Yuri 121
Rix, Simon 166
Robb, John 117

Roberts, Greg 157-58
Robins, Damon 'Des' 144
Rogers, Bev 77
Rogers, Elyse 122
Rossi, Francis 19,22
Rossiter, Martin 108

# S

Salter, Martin 71-72,163
Sanchez, Claudio 168
Savale, Steve Chandrasonic 120
Searle, Jamie 169
Serck, Linda 98
Shannon, Darcus 144
Shaw, Bernie 52-53
Shotton, Tom 163
Simmonds, Paul 85
Simon, Screamin' Scott 14
Smallwood, Rod 26,35,58,60,160
Smith, Dan 168
Smith, Paul 157
Smith, Tom 116
Snider, Des 61
Sonofagun, Rutger 96
Spike 80
Squier, Billy 58
Stanway, Mark 51,74
Stein, Juanita 171
Stephens, Huw 116,158
Sterns, Kreg 110
Stewart, Eric 26
Stewart, Greig 170
Stockdale, Andrew 170
Storace, Marc 52
Story, Riz 138-39
Stringfellow, Ken 101, 115
Stuart, Dan 82
Substance, Markee 137
Sutherland, Gavin 19
Swinnerton, Matthew 157
Sykes, John 64
Symons, Dan 139

# T

Tannen, Amanda 149

Tapper, Michael 158
Tarrie B 126
Tatler, Brian 61
Taylor, Jo
Teckham, Chris 123
Telford, Bush 80
Tellum, Kirstin 88
Terri 133
Thames Valley Police 164
Thomas, Tennessee 171
Thompson, Chris 36
Thompson, Dennis 154
Thunderstick 58-59
Torme, Bernie 46,51
Touter 49
Towns, Colin 49
Trewavas, Peter 61,64-66
Turner, Robert 128,140,146
Turner, Ruby 73

# V

Vickers, Paul 120
Visser, Peter 102
Von Tease, Dita 134

# W

Wagner, Sune Rose 158
Wakeman, Rick 12
Walker, Greg T 61
Walker, Johnnie 148-49
Walsh, Dave 163
Wangford, Hank 84
Wardner, Som 111
Watkins, Ian 152
Watson, Bruce 66
Webb, Billy 158
Wedgewood, Mike 32
Weir, Robb 55
Wentz, Peter 166
Whalley, Boff 101
Wheeler, Tim 112,120
Whelan, Tim 107
Whiley, Jo 157
Whiskas 160
White, Alex 127
Williams, Enid 56

Wiseman, Gary 127
Wisniewski, Tom 122
Wolstenholme, Woolly 26

# X

Xain, P 158

# Y

Yaffa, Sami 66,152
Yan 143